PRINTING ON FABRIC

Techniques with Screens, Stencils, Inks, and Dyes

PRINTING ON FABRIC

Techniques with Screens, Stencils, Inks, and Dyes

Jen Swearington

LARK CRAFTS

Asheville

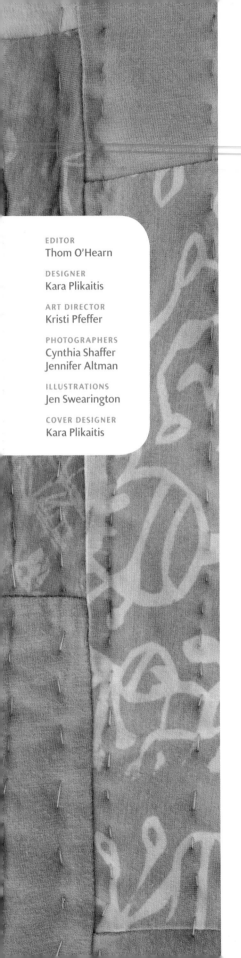

EDITOR
Thom O'Hearn

DESIGNER
Kara Plikaitis

ART DIRECTOR
Kristi Pfeffer

PHOTOGRAPHERS
Cynthia Shaffer
Jennifer Altman

ILLUSTRATIONS
Jen Swearington

COVER DESIGNER
Kara Plikaitis

LARK CRAFTS
An Imprint of Sterling Publishing
387 Park Avenue South
New York, NY 10016

ISBN 978-1-4547-0394-5

Library of Congress Cataloging-in-Publication Data

Swearington, Jen.
  Printing on fabric : techniques with screens, stencils, inks,
and dyes / Jen Swearington. – First Edition.
    pages cm
  Includes index.
  ISBN 978-1-4547-0394-5 (alk. paper)
  1. Textile printing. I. Title.
  TT852.S94 2013
  746.6'2–dc23
                                    2012006729

Distributed in Canada by Sterling Publishing
c/o Canadian Manda Group, 165 Dufferin Street
Toronto, Ontario, Canada M6K 3H6
Distributed in the United Kingdom by GMC Distribution Services
Castle Place, 166 High Street, Lewes, East Sussex, England BN7 1XU
Distributed in Australia by Capricorn Link (Australia) Pty. Ltd.
P.O. Box 704, Windsor, NSW 2756, Australia

For information about custom editions, special sales, and premium and corporate purchases, please contact Sterling Special Sales at 800-805-5489 or specialsales@sterlingpublishing.com.

Email academic@larkbooks.com for information about desk and examination copies. The complete policy can be found at larkcrafts.com.

Manufactured in China

2 4 6 8 10 9 7 5 3 1

larkcrafts.com

CONTENTS

INTRODUCTION

I was in an introductory surface design class when I pulled my first print, lifted the screen off the fabric, and whispered, "Wow." Suddenly, I realized I could take imagery from my sketchbook pages, travel journals, and even found objects to create new stories on fabric. Many years, hundreds of screens, and thousands of yards of silk later, my studio business has thrived by doing exactly that.

Whether you're an experienced quilter, a new sewer, a graphic artist—or if you just want to bring new life to some old threads—I'll show you how to translate your ideas into prints on fabric. Through various modes of printing, from the quick and spontaneous cutting of contact paper stencils to the more methodical marking of half-drop repeats, you'll learn all sorts of new techniques. Whether you want to work small or large, invest a little time and money or a lot, this book will be your go-to guide to do it all.

Like any other hands-on process, printing on fabric involves trial and error. What you find in this book is the result of years of learning and a whole lot of experimentation and practice. While you work, use your senses to make observations, take notes, and improve on your results. At the same time, remember that imperfections can be beautiful, and that mistakes are often the springboard for new discoveries. Feel free to use imagery—both the ones provided and your own—beyond your original project idea. (For example, I've printed that bike on page 122 on a batch of silk scarves, half a dozen women's tees, and my kitchen curtains.) With a little imagination, you will start to see your own surroundings as ripe fields for compelling imagery, too.

Once you start printing, it won't be long before you find yourself excitedly buying blank shirts or stripping your bed sheets and pinning them down to print. Say goodbye to the bland, so long to the ho-hum, and give a great big hello to this very versatile and straightforward process. Soon, you'll be lifting your own screen off the fabric and saying, "Wow!"

CHAPTER 1

IMAGERY, COLOR, INK, AND FABRIC

Thinking about all the possibilities of screenprinting can be thrilling, and even overwhelming! If you have an open mind and a keen sense of observation, you can find inspiration for amazing prints and patterns just about anywhere. There are so many opportunities for new designs, from surprising details in vacation photos to more traditional sources of visual material (like line drawings and clip art). But the choice of ink and fabric can be just as important as the choice of imagery. In this chapter, you'll learn all about these design decisions and how they relate to your eventual print.

WHAT TO PRINT

Whether you plan to make low-tech resists or highly detailed prints using emulsion, in this book you will almost always be using a screen to facilitate the transfer process. So what kind of artwork works best for screenprinting? It's simple: whether you are working with line drawings, clip art, text, or photography, the artwork should make for a clean, crisp stencil. You want high-contrast blacks and whites; you should avoid a lot of subtle grays and midtones. But that doesn't mean your stencil has to be primitive or crude—quite the opposite! It can have a lot of exquisite detail.

Positive and Negative

When considering artwork for printing, you want to think about the *positive*—the area that will print. What you draw is what will print, whether you are making transparencies, cutting black-paper stencils, or typing out text. But if you are making stencils, these block the areas that print, so they are the *negative*. To get an idea of what process works with each, check out Low-Tech Prints on page 36.

Consider Screen Size

Consider what you would like to print and think of the end use. Will your average image fit on a sheet of copy paper for printing tees or span the width of fabric right off the bolt? Your image size is dependent on the size of your screen's print window, the area of mesh left in the middle after taping the screen. If you are just ordering and purchasing your screens, you can guesstimate the approximate print window size. Everybody tapes a little differently, so I would use a rough guess that the dimensions of the print window will be about 6 to 10 inches (15.2 to 25.4 cm) smaller than the outside dimensions of the frame. Keep in mind that you can print a small image in the middle of a large screen, no problem, **A** but you can't fit a large design on too small of a screen. **B** When in doubt, get a little larger screen since it's better to have extra room for taping and printing than having to print teeny stencils every time.

A

B

Images

I tend to think of images as representational of things in the real world: a maple leaf, a hot air balloon, a red-tailed fox, or the king of hearts. By far my favorite things to print, images tell stories, infusing the material with meaning and content and narrative. When I use imagery out of my sketchbooks to make screens, they are generally crammed together, so I put multiple images on a screen. It's also important to me to conserve the fine detail of the line drawings, so I don't enlarge them very much. I fit what I can in a print window format, but I enjoy mixing the different sketches to make a panoramic pattern module, always in a rectangle.

Motifs

In classical music, a *leitmotif* is a small group of notes, a miniature melody repeated and varied through a composition, giving it unity. Think of "da da da dum" in Beethoven's Fifth Symphony, repeated throughout the piece, bounced around the composition and sections of the orchestra. Similarly, a *motif* is a decorative design element; it can be representational or abstract. Think of motifs with historical and cultural references: a fleur-de-lis, a paisley, and more abstract motifs such as a circle made up of dotted lines, a diamond, a square, an ellipse.

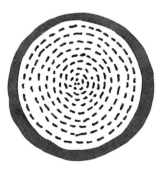

COLOR BASICS

When I teach adults to screenprint for the first time, they almost always ask, "What color should I use?" even if they are printing on plain white T-shirts. I've noticed that kids never experience this dilemma. Kids don't overthink it; they go for it. When you pull a print, you will know right away whether the color works. It's intuitive.

The Color Wheel

Whether you are working with inks or dyes, fabric or paper, opaque or transparent media, the principles of color theory all work the same. It doesn't matter how you blend the colors either. Paint on paper, drops of color concentrate in ink extender, dye solutions, or even layering translucent fabrics—the color-mixing principles stay the same while the range of variations becomes infinite. As you work and play with color, you will see your own palettes evolving, growing more sophisticated and nuanced. You can refer to the color wheel I've illustrated for this book, or you can play around with making your own.

Primary Colors

The largest circles are the primary colors: red, blue, and yellow. These three, along with black and white, are the ingredients for mixing all other colors. Primary colors cannot be mixed from other colors. But why are there so many different yellows, reds, and blues? In paint, inks, and dyes, just like in the real world, there isn't just one yellow. In a typical morning, I see the yellow of an egg yolk, of a dandelion, of a Golden Delicious apple, of a street sign, of my cat Jasper's eyes, and on and on. Each of these yellows is just a little bit different from the next and wonderful in its own way. Similarly, the textile ink colors available in one catalog run the gamut of options. There's brilliant yellow, lemon yellow, golden yellow, and several more yellows to boot.

Mix any of them with some kind of red, whether it's carmine red, bright red, deep red, barn red, or magenta, and chances are pretty good that you will still get some kind of orange. So I encourage you to experiment with different primaries; this will increase your range and your understanding of color. And even though you are just learning basic color theory, your own individual palette will become more nuanced and sophisticated with experience.

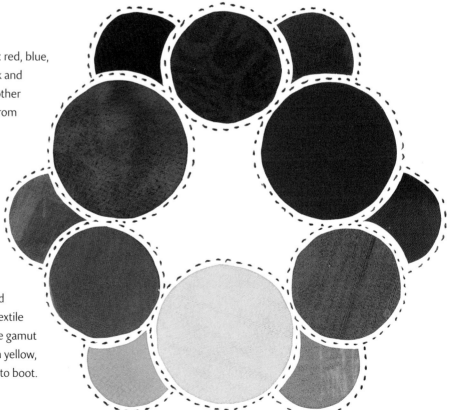

Secondary and Tertiary Colors

The next three circles are the secondary colors, made by mixing two primaries. These are purple, green, and orange. Purple is made from red and blue, green is made from blue and yellow, and orange is made from yellow and red. When a secondary color is mixed with the primary color next to it, they make the outer row: the tertiary colors of red-purple, blue-purple, blue-green, yellow-green, yellow-orange, and red-orange. I'm sure you can figure out by their names what colors were mixed to make each of them.

Generally, red, orange, and yellow are considered warm. Warm colors are energizing and seem to advance from the surface. Green, blue, and purple are considered cool, calming and recede back into the surface.

Build a Brighter Color Wheel

Okay, red, blue, and yellow, in theory, are the primaries for mixing all colors. They make perfect sense and work just fine. But would you like your printing palette to be just a little brighter and livelier? Simply substitute turquoise for blue and magenta for red. Turquoise is basically cyan, and magenta is a cool red that leans a little toward bright pink and purple. By swapping out red and blue, you are adjusting your palette from theory colors to practical printing colors, following the model the of the CMYK palette used for printing on paper and fabric. CMYK stands for cyan, magenta, yellow, and key (black). Since this is a subtractive process, with each color taking brightness from a white surface, changing out a couple of primary colors will yield a brighter color wheel and therefore more vivid palettes.

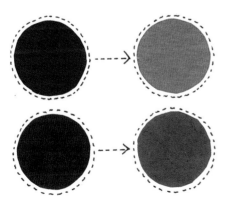

Three Popular Color Schemes

COMPLEMENTARY COLORS: Want to make a color pop right off the page? Pair it with its complement! Colors across from each other on the color wheel are complements: blue with orange, red-orange with blue-green, blue-violet with yellow-orange, and so on. Play with keeping one color muted by mixing in a little black, white, or—yes—even a little of the complement, while keeping the other one pure and intense. While a common reference for pairing complements red and green is a Christmas palette, think again! This complementary scheme of five colors relates more to a patch of strawberries in June than the holiday season.

MONOCHROMATIC COLORS: Want to get a lot of bang out of one color buck? Work with one color and its variations of tints and shades—even set it off against bits of pure black and white. Check out the monochromatic discharge-printed Butterfly Chair Cover on page 113.

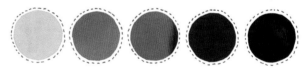

ANALOGOUS COLORS: Want a sense of harmony? Select colors next to each other on the color wheel, along with their variations. The yellow-orange to red-orange palette can evoke a blazing sunset over a desert landscape. Another analogous palette contains the shades of golden yellow, yellow-green, green, and blue, in the light field of the Night and Day Quilt on page 142.

More Mixing

Mixing in a little complement to a color is a painterly method of making deeper, darker colors without resorting to black or gray, which I think can dull and deaden colors. Keep it lively! Adding white to a color makes it a *tint* while adding black to a color makes it a *shade.* Adding gray makes it a *tone*—less and less saturated and more and more neutral.

Now that we've explored color in theory, let's consider color practice: working with inks and other colorants out of their jars and on the fabric.

JUMP-START YOUR CREATIVITY

Make a simple viewfinder frame with two L-shaped pieces of paper as shown. As magazines, catalogs, and old photos pile up, use your viewfinder to isolate areas of color, pattern, and details that you like. Then trace or cut out the areas and put them in your sketchbook with notes for current or future projects. This is a great way to play with color to break out of your usual palette, as well as to explore composition and arrangement.

TEXTILE INKS, OTHER COLORANTS, AND BASE EXTENDERS

For printing on fabric, I use a lot of water-based inks. You will be amazed how easy they are to mix and print with. They are also easily heat-set so they are permanent, and you can wash what you print without the design fading or peeling off. Textile inks are available in so many varieties, both premixed and in a simple mixing system, from transparent to opaque, pearlescent, to metallic, puffy, even fluorescent and glow in the dark! Once you're comfortable with printing with textile inks, you can move on to chemical colorants: dyes and color removers. These are a little more technical, but they offer another world of possibilities in depth and subtlety. We'll get into working with these heavy hitters later on in chapter 6.

Textile Inks

Textile printing inks, sometimes called textile paints, are designed to adhere to fabrics so they are permanent through washing and wearing. The whole system is water based, low odor, and easy to mix and use. But be careful to get the right stuff! Some textile paints are thin and runny, formulated for the wet-on-wet watercolor effects of silk painting. If you get confused about what to buy, most products state their use on their labels or product descriptions. Look for descriptions like "for screenprinting, stenciling, and block printing on fabric," or something along those lines. Avoid products with descriptions like, "for hand painting, silk painting, or spraying." And it should be called *ink* or *paint* and not *dye*, which is very different and requires a much more involved setting process that we'll get into in chapter 6.

Premixed textile inks have a thick, puddinglike consistency for printing and are available in a dazzling array of colors, opacities, and novelty finishes. You may want to start with a few basic primary colors to mix—it is very straightforward. Or just buy some that work for you without mixing. I'm easily seduced by all the shiny, happy pearlescent colors!

Color Concentrates

If the possibilities found in premixed textile inks aren't enough, color concentrates and an array of base extenders will let you mix pretty much anything you can dream up. Color concentrate pigments are pure, intense, finely ground particles of color in a water-based suspension. These potent potions are too thin and runny to screenprint with on their own; they would bleed and run all over the fabric! So you'll need to mix the color with a base extender—a thick, colorless paint body—to make your own textile ink. You can vary the amount of color mixed into the extender to create pale, medium, or dark shades of ink, drop by powerful little drop. This system gives maximum flexibility in color choice, consistency, opacity, sheen, and texture. There is no tricky chemistry, cooking, or timing involved; you just mix up anything you like, spoon it onto your screen, and print.

Even when you mix your own inks from color concentrates and extenders, you must heat-set them with an iron or other heat source so the ink doesn't come out in the wash. After heat-setting, always allow the print to cure at least a week before washing. (This is a good reason to prewash your fabrics!)

Base Extenders

Different extenders each have their own wonderful properties, and it is fun to play, experiment, and layer the endless formulas of concoctions you can mix up.

TRANSPARENT EXTENDER: This extender is best for printing on light fabric, painting a base layer, and for achieving a subtle layered effect. Like its name implies, transparent extender allows the color or pattern on which it's printed to show through. So if you print with color and transparent extender on dark or brightly patterned fabric, it would not hide the fabric underneath but blend with it; your image would not stand out from the background with much contrast. A

OPAQUE EXTENDER: An opaque extender is the best kind for printing light color on dark fabric, as it is designed to obscure the color or pattern on which it is printed. It can also be used on light fabrics, though the heavier consistency can feel a little more stiff than transparent. I use opaque extender for T-shirts to achieve a high-contrast, bold image. B

PEARLESCENT EXTENDER: This type of extender is fun for giving a color a shiny, pearly finish. I call it "print candy." C

PUFF EXTENDER: Now this one is just plain fun! With a little heat, it creates a textured, raised printed image, combining the crisp imagery of screenprinting with the textural depth of puffy goodness. Down with the gloppy old puff paints dribbled out of squeeze bottles (though they probably are still around somewhere)! Screenprinting puff extender is a far more fascinating, and less dated, alternative, as you can see in my Puffy Cloud Pillows at right. D

Dyes and Color Removers

I love dyeing fabric and hand dye all the silk fabrics in my Jennythreads production line. In this book we'll work with fiber reactive dyes, which are extremely user friendly and widely popular with hobbyists and professionals alike. Dyes and color removers react with fabric fibers at the molecular level, and printing with each of them is a slightly more complicated chemical process than printing with textile inks. The richness and subtlety achieved with dye printing, however, is unmatched by textile inks, which act more like paint on the surface of the fabric.

Color removers are also known as *discharge agents*. Think of them not exactly as color erasers, but color transformers. When they are applied to dyed fabrics, they react with the dye molecules to create lighter colors. The three we will be using are premixed discharge paste, thiourea dioxide (thiox), and good old household chlorine bleach (again, this will be covered in detail in chapter 6).

Other Paints and Colorants

The mechanics of screenprinting allow you to print anything you can squish through the stencil. So theoretically, you can print peanut butter (creamy, not chunky!) and jelly (no seeds) onto a giant piece of toast. More realistically, I know ceramic artists who screenprint slip onto clay. In a pinch, I've used acrylic paint for my own work—though I made sure to wash the screen out immediately after printing since it dries so fast.

BEWARE OF MYSTERY INK

Once I made several screens for a friend who took them home and printed with some oil-based or enamel paint she had lying around, and, sadly, she clogged up all of her brand-new screens on the first print and threw every single one in the trash. So if you are going to print with some mystery ink you found under the basement stairs or on clearance at the art supply store, test it first to be sure it will wash out of your screen. If the label says it's acrylic, latex, or water based, be sure it dissolves in water and dries slowly so you to have time to rinse it. If it's oil based, make sure that you have the solvent to dissolve it and that the solvent doesn't damage your screen or stencil.

MIX CUSTOM TEXTILE INKS

If you are printing with premixed textile inks right out of the jar, you're ready to print. But you may want a color that doesn't come straight out of the jar. Lucky for us, textile inks can be mixed like any other type of paint. So if you have red and yellow and want to make orange, it's fine to mix right out of the two jars. But what if you don't have premixed textile inks? Well, if you've got a few color concentrates over here and some extender over there, you will need to mix up a batch of ink no matter what color you want to print with. So let's get started!

YOU WILL NEED:

Extender

Measuring cup

Small mixing container with lid

Eyedropper

Color concentrate

Spoon or spatula

INSTRUCTIONS:

1   Spoon about 4 ounces ($^1/_2$ cup) of extender into your mixing container.

2   Add the color concentrate drop by drop (it's very intense) and stir. As you might expect, less concentrate makes paler colors; more concentrate makes darker colors. You can make new colors by combining drops of different colors in the mix. **A**

3   Put the lid on the mixing container until you are ready to print. Mixed textile inks last for months as long as they are in an airtight container, and they do not have to be refrigerated. As long as it is in a tightly sealed container, it should not dry out. If a few months have gone by and you discover it has dried to a solid block, just toss it; you can't revive it.

A

FABRICS AND OTHER SUBSTRATES

The textile inks we'll be using are easy to print on most fabrics. If the end use does not involve washing, I encourage you to experiment with any substrate material that captures your imagination! But we are working on fabric, and for most applications, it is something that will eventually be laundered, so it is best to get into the habit of prewashing fabrics in hot water before printing on them. Washing fabrics in hot water with a little bit of mild detergent (by hand or machine) and drying them on high heat will make sure they shrink as much as they ever will—which is better than having them shrink and distort after investing all your hard work.

Fabric Structures

When considering a fabric to print on and dye, it's helpful to have a basic understanding of its structure—how the fiber was made (woven, knit, or felted) and its fiber content (what raw material it is made of). Knowing the fiber content will be especially important when you get into printing with dyes and color removers because they work by chemical reaction with the specific materials.

WOVEN FABRICS: If you got the kit to make your own pot holders on a little plastic loom when you were a kid, you were weaving. Over, under, over, under, pulling a loop with a hook through rows of stretchy bands. Sound familiar? Commercially produced woven fabrics are constructed in the same way on a much larger loom than the little red plastic one, with warp threads running vertically and weft threads interlaced between them horizontally. Along the sides of the fabric is the selvage, a prefinished border made where the weft threads wrap around the warp and change direction. Woven fabrics are stiff and stable, do not have much stretch, and unravel when cut. Think denim overalls, crisp cotton bedsheets, an oxford shirt, or a linen tablecloth. Woven fabrics are an optimal choice for beginning screenprinting because they offer a smooth, stable print material surface.

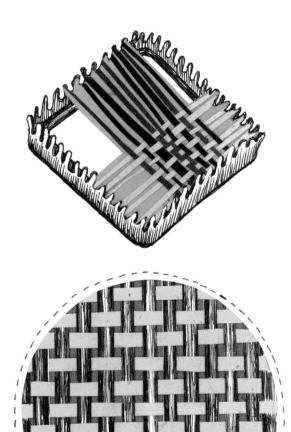

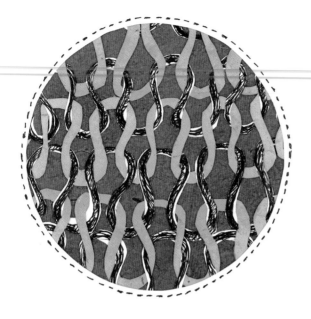 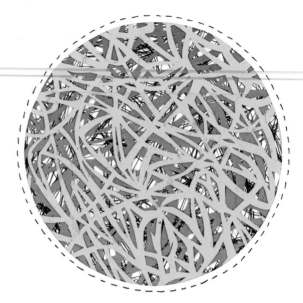

KNIT FABRICS: Knit fabrics are created with one continuous thread looped around itself in a pattern. They can be knit in a flat sheet or a continuous tube; that's why many T-shirts don't have side seams. Knits have lots of stretch, do not unravel when cut, and are used widely in apparel. Think of a cozy hand-knitted baby blanket, track suits, socks and hosiery, and of course, T-shirts. Smooth jersey knits and heavier sweatshirt knits are terrific to print on, while chunky, bumpy-textured, cable-knit sweaters are not.

FELTED FABRICS: Have you ever accidentally shrunk a wool sweater in the wash? Then you have felted. Felted fabrics are formed when fibers, most commonly wool, mesh together, forming a tightly tangled material that cannot be stretched out or undone. If you were to look at a wool fiber under a microscope, you would see its surface is covered with tiny scales. With heat and agitation (and strong alkali found in some detergents) the scales lift and lock together with their nearest neighbors. Felt is perfect for printing and appliqué, since it is easy to stitch through and can be easily cut into shapes that do not fray or curl—much like working with thick paper. If you need to prewash wool and you want to keep it from felting into a miniature version of itself, wash it by hand. Be sure to use cold water and mild detergent, and don't agitate it too much. Rinse it well and lay it flat on a towel, roll up the towel and squeeze the water out (I stomp on it), remove the wool item, and let it air-dry.

Fiber Content

Fiber content is simply what raw material the fabric is made from: cotton, polyester, silk, rayon, wool, and so on. When printing with textile inks, fiber content does not make much difference. When you get into dyeing fabric, however, knowing the fiber content becomes far more important.

Fibers come from three major sources: plants, animals, and synthetic sources. Both plant- and animal-based fibers are considered natural fibers, while synthetics are man-made concoctions created in the laboratory or as by-products of industrial processes. Here are some examples of each.

- Plant-based fibers (cellulose): cotton, linen, hemp, bamboo, soy, rayon
- Animal-based fibers (protein): silk, wool, cashmere, yak down, angora
- Synthetic fibers: polyester, nylon, spandex, PET (recycled plastic bottles)

When you're out shopping at the fabric store, you will inevitably run into lots of fabric blends; this is when fibers are mixed together to create new hybrid fabrics. For my clothing line, I work with natural fiber fabrics that have a small percentage of synthetic material such as spandex, which add "stretchy" properties that make my pieces much more wearable and user friendly without compromising their ability to be dyed.

Other Substrates: Paper and Wood

The focus of this book is printing on fabric, but I also have fun playing around with printing on other porous materials such as paper and wood, and once you have gotten comfortable with fabric printing, I encourage you to experiment on these other materials as well. Since textile paints are heat-set with an iron, it is just as easy to print and heat-set on paper or even on wood. If you'd like to print on paper, you don't necessarily need a padded surface. You can tape the corners of the paper to your regular work-table. Keep in mind that paper is not nearly as absorbent as fabric; as a result, you'll need to use less ink so it doesn't smear. I've screenprinted imagery on wood in some mixed media pieces, and wood is not absorbent like fabric. That means it is even more challenging not to smear too much ink when printing. It just takes a little practice and experi-mentation. To protect the printed wood surface, seal it with a couple coats of shellac or polyurethane.

THE BURN AND BLEACH TESTS FOR MYSTERY FABRICS

So, you are at the fabric store and find a terrific fabric, but is it a natural fiber that can be dyed or a synthetic that can't? Here's an easy test, you'll just need a lighter or book of matches. Ask for a small swatch of the fabric and take it outside. Fray a few threads of the fabric, light them with the lighter, and watch how they burn. Natural fibers burn like paper, turning black and then flaking off. Synthetics, which are essentially plastics, melt off into a hard bead.

You can also test the fabric color's ability to be discharged. Bring a little container of bleach and a cotton swab, apply it to an area of the swatch that you didn't set on fire, and see if the bleach lightens the color within a few minutes. Keep in mind that bleach is a more powerful color remover than discharge paste or thiourea dioxide, so if you are planning to use either of them on the fabric, bring a swatch home to test.

TIP *Here's a terrific trick for cutting most woven fabrics: snip and tear. If you don't trust yourself to cut it in a nice straight line, the fabric does it for you. Simply use scissors and snip about an inch (2.5 cm) at the length you'd like to cut, and then pull it apart. The fabric tears in a straight line at a neat 90° from the selvage.*

CHAPTER 2

GETTING STARTED

Ladies and gentlemen, this is the chapter where the magic happens. I am thrilled to show you how easy it is to pull your first print. You'll soon see that you don't need a full-sized studio, or even a studio at all. Really, there are only a few supplies standing between you and a print. But I'm warning you, printing is addictive—after you create just one print, you'll be hooked. I've seen it happen to the best of them! Soon you'll be rummaging through your closet and searching around the room for your next blank canvas.

SETTING UP YOUR STUDIO

A fabric-printing studio can look reminiscent of home economics class with all the domestic tools about. But that's a nice thing, too! Rounding up a few useful items around the house beats having to acquire a ton of specialty equipment.

Basic Tools

IRON AND IRONING BOARD: An iron is indispensable in the studio for heat-setting your textile inks after printing, as well as occasionally straightening out unruly fabrics. It doesn't have to be fancy! A cheap iron or one from the thrift store is fine. And if you don't have room for a full ironing board, a little travel-size board is fine, or even a towel folded in half on the table works. Just be careful not to iron on your vinyl printing surface—it could melt! Also, if your iron doesn't have an automatic shutoff feature, make some sort of reminder to shut it off yourself, whether a note by the door or an alarm on your phone.

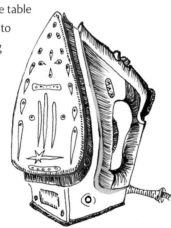

PINS AND PINCUSHION:
T-pins are commonly used in pinning fabric down to the print table, but I personally find T-pins clunky, barbaric, and unnecessary. The top bar of the T can resist ink from reaching the fabric and leave an unprinted line. Often fabric gets caught in the bend of the T, and T-pins are prone to rust. I prefer simple glass-ball-head pins. Though they are not as sturdy, they are fine enough to not leave holes in the fabric, the ball head is easy to find and pull out after printing (even while wearing gloves), and they do not get tangled in the fabric.

Stick your pins in a pincushion rather than leaving them in the little plastic box they come in. They are easier to pull, put back, and find while you are working.

HAIR DRYER: Freshly printed textile inks won't dry faster just because you stare them down really hard, so save your sanity and grab the hair dryer from the bathroom to speed things along. If you are working on a small printing area and the real estate is valuable, or if you are printing yardage, which takes four separate sessions of waiting for ink to dry, you'll be so glad you have it. Also, keep an extension cord nearby so your dryer will reach the prints!

STAPLE GUN AND STAPLES: If you are stretching your own screen or building your own printing board, you will need a good staple gun. I gave up the palm-blistering, conventional-style staple gun years ago. I have a strong preference for the more ergonomically designed staple guns; they're usually not much different in price and they're much more hand friendly. Look for a gun where the staples come out of the end that you push. With this type, you can lean into it instead of squeezing, so you don't need monstrous muscled hands to operate it, and you won't wind up with raw, blistered fingers after stretching one screen. Oh, and forget the corded models, too.

Be sure to get staples that are made to go in your particular staple gun. I like 3/8-inch (.95 cm) staples for screenprinting frames. I've found 1/4-inch (.6 cm) ones don't sink into the wood enough and tend to pull out easily, and 1/2-inch (1.3 cm) staples don't seem to penetrate into the wood and end up protruding from the surface.

HAMMER: If you've got use for a staple gun, you'll need a hammer to pound down any staples that stick up a little bit to make a flush, flat surface.

TAPE: Masking tape is great for patching a leaky stencil or taping paper down to the table to print. And duct tape is my choice for taping screens. It is used to create the print window of the screen and to allow room for an *ink reservoir*, the starting point for pulling the ink across the stencil. Pick up a big roll at the hardware store; the little one won't be enough. These days, the duct tape color selection is dazzling, so pick out something fun! Like I mentioned above, you need to tape your screen before applying the stencil and prints, so check out Taping Your Screen on page 28.

BROWN KRAFT PAPER: Handy-dandy brown kraft paper is cheap, sturdy, and indispensable in the studio. You can get a 140-foot (42.7 m) roll of it at the home improvement store for less than 15 bucks. It has multiple uses in my studio: as a reusable insert inside T-shirts while printing, as pressing paper for ironing things with fresh ink, and even as a dress pattern template.

FABRIC SHEARS: I strictly prohibit cutting anything but fabric with my fabric shears. Since I cut lots and lots of garments from patterns, I prefer the spring-loaded fabric shears; they reduce hand fatigue by half.

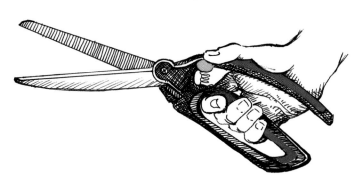

SCISSORS: Don't wear out your fabric shears by cutting paper, duct tape, and other no-no's. Get a cheap pair of scissors for everything but fabric, and your shears will last for years.

SEWING KIT: Once you get into printing on fabric, you'll want to start making things out of it, so you'll need the sewing basics: needle, thread, your pins and pincushion, and one of my best little friends, a seam ripper. A dressmaker's measuring tape is terrific for measuring fabric yardage, screens, people, anything, and you can wear it around your neck or keep it in your apron pocket. I also really like spring-tensioned fabric snips, handy for snipping threads and for reverse appliqué in sewing.

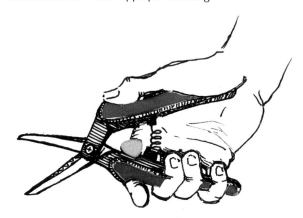

BUCKETS: I like small 1- and 2-gallon (3.8 and 7.8 liters) buckets for prewashing new fabric and for washing and rinsing dyed and printed fabric pieces in the sink, especially if you don't have a washer or enough to run a full load.

Safety Gear

I'm not your mom, but I urge you to take care of yourself while working and to keep your workspace clean. At right is how I look, suited up and ready to print, in my apron, gloves, and respirator.

GLOVES: I recommend wearing long rubber nitrile or dishwashing gloves that cover your wrists and forearms while mixing and printing; they last for weeks, and you still have decent dexterity while wearing them. Avoid wearing disposable surgical gloves. They don't cover your wrists or arms, they are hard to take on and off while printing, and they don't offer protection against hot water and steam. Plus you'd blaze through a dozen in one afternoon of printing.

RESPIRATOR: Many products, such as textile paints, are odorless and nontoxic. Color removal agents such as chlorine bleach and thiox, on the other hand, are more toxic and emit noxious fumes. You will need to wear a respirator with cartridges for vapors when working with them. A respirator is a mask that covers the mouth and nose, with straps that go around your head. It has two replaceable filter cartridges that keep nasty fumes and unpleasant odors from entering the mask. Keep your respirator in a sealed plastic bag when you are not using it; this extends the life of the filter cartridges. A respirator with vapor filter cartridges will also keep out dust and powdered dye particles so you won't need an additional dust mask.

DUST MASK: For mixing powdered dyes, you'll need to wear at least a dust mask like the kind used for sanding drywall if you don't have a respirator. Pick one up at the hardware store. Dyes are made up of tiny particles that fly in the air and eventually into your lungs. Once they are mixed with water, they are in a more stable form and no longer airborne, so you can take off the mask once they are in solution.

YOUR STUDIO

Studio can seem like a heavy-duty word. It can sound artsy and pretentious, but it is just a name for a place where you can be productive and creative. You don't have to have a fancy loft above an art gallery to screenprint fabric. In my first apartment after graduate school, I slept in the dining room and turned its one bedroom into my studio, which had nothing but a small printing board on sawhorses, and I did most of my work crawling around on the floor. At least I could go into the room to work and then close the door behind me on my way out. But for many creative people, even having a whole room in which to work can be a luxury. If you don't have the space for a dedicated studio, you can still create a portable, stash-away workspace, with your materials and tools organized and ready for you when inspiration strikes. I'll show you on page 30 how to build a simple printing board that can be stowed when not in use.

APRON: A canvas work apron is very useful when printing. You'll see just how useful when leaning over the table to print and finding you've just transferred the ink to your own shirt. Believe it or not, one summer day, I was ironing a print wearing no apron, not paying close attention and actually burned my skin right next to my belly button with the edge of the iron! Ridiculous *and* true. And in graduate school, I had a collection of adorable 1950s waist aprons that I wore while working in the studio. They were super cute but made from lightweight fabric and not much protection against printing ink, so even though I wore an apron, all my clothes had stains on them—especially across the waist—from leaning over the table to print. Those aprons have long gone into the scrap bin. If you ever take a class at one of the great American craft schools like Arrowmont, Penland, or Haystack, pick up a souvenir apron; that's what I wear. I love wiping my gloved hands on my apron without looking around for a towel, plus putting on an apron feels very official. Ready to work!

MATERIAL SAFETY DATA SHEET (MSDS): If you are not sure of the hazards of working with a particular chemical, you can look up its MSDS, or material safety data sheet. The MSDS lists facts about a material such as whether it is nontoxic, ingredients that can be hazardous if misused, and four major data categories: physical, fire and explosive, reactivity, and health effects. It tells you what precautions you need to take, safety gear you should wear, and how to deal with the chemical in an emergency. The major dye supply houses offer MSDS sheets for their products free for downloading on their websites. Many studios (including mine) keep a binder of MSDS information for all chemicals in-house; it can provide helpful information to first responders in case of emergency.

The Screen

The screen is comprised of two components: the mesh and the frame. Screens are usually purchased preassembled and stretched. You can build your own frames out of pressure-treated lumber, but the savings are pretty minimal. What has worked best for me is to pay for a few new prestretched wooden screens. Then, when the mesh wears out, I cut it out of the frame and stretch new mesh. I am still reusing my first frames from 1998.

All screens—prestretched or do-it-yourself—need to be taped before printing. For a tutorial on this process, see Taping Your Screen, page 28.

THE MESH: The mesh is the "screen" in screenprinting. It is the surface where you block out one area and leave another porous, creating the printed design. The mesh is generally a plain-woven, synthetic fabric made up of threads running horizontally and vertically. Through this fine grid of tiny holes, ink or paint is pushed with the squeegee onto the fabric, paper, or other substrate being printed. Traditionally silk was used (hence the more antiquated term *silk screen*), but silk loses its tension over time and cannot hold up to many of the solvents and chemicals used in modern processes. For example, if you printed thickened bleach through a silken screen, the bleach would break down the silk fibers, dissolving and shredding your screen as you print! That's a bad studio day.

Screenprinting mesh is available in different widths, just like in fabric yardage. I buy the widest available yardage to have more flexibility when covering multiple frames. Since the mesh is a plain-weave fabric, it can be measured, snipped with scissors, and then ripped by hand; it will tear in a straight line at a 90° angle, and you will have a straight-cut piece to stretch on your frame.

Mesh count is the other variable to consider when buying mesh. Basically, it is the number of threads per inch (2.5 cm), but it can be thought of as the resolution (similar to dpi or pixel count) of your screen. The higher the number, the finer the mesh. High numbers are optimal if you are going for very fine detail or printing on paper.

Higher mesh count is usually more expensive, too. Since fabric has a rougher texture than most paper, you don't have to buy the top of the line; the really high detail you're paying for will just get lost when it's transferred onto the fabric. I go with a midrange thread count, anything from around 70 to 110 threads per inch (2.5 cm).

Most mesh is white in color and works fine for any printing application. However, if you plan to make a lot of screens using photo emulsion with very fine detail, I recommend getting yellow- or orange-toned screen mesh. This reduces the light that is bounced around the white reflective fibers during exposure and gives you an even crisper image.

THE FRAME: Commercially made printing screens are very sturdy and durable. Unless you are handy, strong, and have some basic woodworking equipment, it is difficult to match the commercial ones in strength and stability—especially with medium to large frames. I like wooden frames because they can be stapled, since I like to restretch them myself. Another alternative is aluminum frames, which are strong, lightweight, and impervious to water. The downside of aluminum is that they must be restretched professionally. On the quicker and flimsier side, I have tried snapping together a frame of painter's stretcher strips, but these warp easily under the pressure of stretching the screen and do not hold up well to water. I would recommend this alternative only when making a very small frame (outside dimensions of 12 inches [30.5 cm] or smaller) for quick experiments or making exposure test swatches for photo emulsion (see page 64).

Specialty Screenprinting Tools

SQUEEGEE: A squeegee is a rigid blade that is used to push your medium (in our case that's usually textile paint) through the screen mesh and onto the fabric. Squeegees are sold in different widths, and traditionally your squeegee should be approximately the width of your screen's print window. My first squeegee was 12 inches (30.5 cm) wide, which I found heavy and bulky to manipulate, so I eventually sawed it into two smaller squeegees: one 8 inches (20.3 cm) wide and the other 4 inches (10.2 cm) wide. A good size for a beginner is 6 to 8 inches (15.2 to 20.3 cm) wide—you can hold it and pull it with one hand. If you plan to print with large screens, you will want to have a large squeegee that matches the width of your print window. Just keep in mind that larger squeegees will have to be pulled across the screen with both hands.

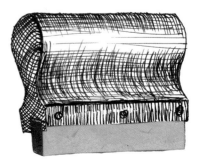

The squeegee's rubber blade has a measured rigidity known as its *durometer*. Basically, this means the lower the number, the softer the blade. So 55 is quite soft, whereas 95 is hard. Somewhere in the 65 to 75 range is most common for printing textiles by hand. Avoid the "student grade" or "craft" squeegee with a plastic handle and a much thinner, softer blade; it may be slightly less expensive than a wooden handled one, but you will find it is uncomfortable on your hands, and it is prone to bend and warp. I found the most comfortable squeegees have a thick wooden handle with a rubber blade.

DECAL SPREADER: For smaller images and thermal screens, a big wooden squeegee can be cumbersome and clunky. Instead, I like using a small plastic spreader sold at sign shops to apply decals. An old credit card also works well. In a pinch, a square of mat board or foam core will suffice, but it quickly becomes soggy with ink, so you won't get much use out of it.

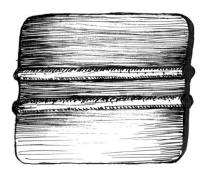

PAINTBRUSHES: I use a small artist's paintbrush for touching up prints where they need a little more ink or for deftly picking up excess.

CUPS, SPOONS, AND SPATULAS: For mixing textile inks, you don't need to measure precisely, so you can round up empty yogurt containers, old spoons, spatulas, and wooden tongue depressors. For small mixing containers, I've found cheap, resealable food containers like dairy containers with lids work just fine. For more exact measuring, use an old set of measuring cups and spoons (and don't bring them back into the kitchen!).

PRINTING SURFACE: This can be as minimal as suits your needs or as large as a dedicated table (see page 31). You will need at least a printing board for most types of printing. If you go this route, set it up on a sturdy table or pair of sawhorses, and make sure it is larger than your table (so that a T-square will rest against the side of it if needed).

Some printers prefer to tape their fabric down to a table and do not bother with a padded surface. This is a personal preference. I print on a padded surface for two reasons: it provides good contact between the screen and fabric, and I can pin the fabric to the table so it stays down when the screen is lifted. Similarly, when I print on existing sewn items, I want the fabric to be taut so ink doesn't collect in the seams. For padding your print surface, I've seen other printers use carpet padding, but I use 1-inch-thick (2.5 cm) foam rubber, available from upholstery and fabric shops. I've had the same piece for about 12 years, and it is showing no signs of wearing out. I like 1-inch (2.5 cm) foam because pins don't hit the bottom and poke into the board, unlike with thinner padding.

For a print-surface covering, I use a sheet of vinyl. I find vinyl is sturdy, easy to pin through, and especially easy to wipe off anything from inks to thickened bleach to—ahem—spilled coffee, and then I don't have to bother with drop cloths. It is available in lots of colors and looks neat and clean.

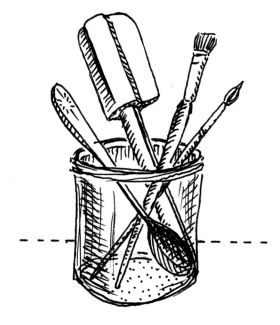

TAPING YOUR SCREEN

Taping your screen is a necessity, but it doesn't take too much time. You'll also get quicker and quicker with every screen you tape. I recommend using duct tape, but blue painter's tape can work in a pinch (it's just a bit less durable so it won't hold up as well).

YOU WILL NEED:

Clean, dry screen

Scissors

Staple gun and ⅜-inch (.95 cm) staples

Hammer

Duct tape

INSTRUCTIONS:

1   Tape the squeegee side. I try to use every square inch of a print window, so I tape narrower borders than most printers. Here's how. On the two long sides, center the strip of tape on the seam between the mesh and the frame so one skinny half is on the mesh and the other is banked up on the frame. On the two short sides, use the full width of the tape (many printers use two widths) on the mesh to create a wider area, known as a *reservoir* or a *well*, where you spoon the ink to pull it with the squeegee and print. Remember to stagger the seams as you go. If the tape strips are a little extra long, just bank them up the side of the frame.

2   Tape the print side. Flip the screen and align strips of tape to face those on the squeegee side along the perimeter of the print window, staggering the seams as you go. Continue to add strips of tape to overlap the previous ones until you cover the print side of the screen. Don't bother taping the sides of the frame. Use the rounded handle of your scissors to burnish the tape and let it cure 24 hours before getting it wet; this will ensure the tape stays adhered through years of use.

STRETCH YOUR SCREEN

When you've completely worn through a screen with a wooden frame, restretch it! All you need is the wood frame and some screen mesh (see page 25). Place the screen frame on a flat, sturdy surface like a worktable or floor. Snip and tear (see the tip on page 19) a piece of mesh to measure a few inches larger than the frame. Center the mesh on the frame and staple it at the center of two opposite sides. Pull the mesh taut from the center outward toward the corners and add a staple on either side of the first staple at 1-inch (2.5 cm) intervals. Repeat this step on the two remaining sides. Continue to pull the mesh and staple, alternating two opposite sides at a time, until you reach the corners. Then trim any excess mesh outside of the screen frame, hammer any protruding staples flat, and tape it.

MAKE A T-SHIRT PRINTING INSERT

If you don't want to pull out a printing board every time you want to print a tee, you can make a simple T-shirt printing template.

YOU WILL NEED:

Piece of cardboard slightly larger than a typical T-shirt

Matching-size piece of 1-inch (2.5 cm) foam or an old bath towel or beach towel

Masking tape, packing tape, or pins

Old pillowcase or sheet of fabric in comparable size

T-shirt

Scrap kraft paper

INSTRUCTIONS:

1 Wrap or roll the foam or towel around the cardboard; this will give your insert some padding for good contact between the tee and the screen. Pay close attention to keeping it neat and wrinkle-free. Secure the foam or towel around the cardboard with tape or pins.

2 Place the padded board inside the pillowcase and tape or pin it tautly on the back to create a smooth surface.

3 Slide the tee over it and insert a sheet of scrap paper behind the area you will print.

4 Once you have printed, pull the tee and the scrap paper backing off the insert together. Leave the scrap paper within the T-shirt so the ink doesn't soak through to the back layer, and set it aside to dry. While it is drying, you can slide your next tee on the insert and print again.

BUILD A SIMPLE PRINT BOARD

Here's how to make a 4 x 4-foot (1.2 x 1.2 m) square printing board. You can modify the size of the board to suit your space and lifestyle, just make sure the covering material is at least 6 inches (15.2 cm) larger than the overall board size, allowing you 3 inches (7.6 cm) extra material on each side to wrap it around and staple. I recommend making your board as big as you can handle and store; it's always nice to have extra print space rather than not enough. A printing board can be placed on a table or set of sawhorses, which are also collapsible, to print and then put away when not in use.

YOU WILL NEED:

1 sheet of vinyl 6 inches (15.2 cm) larger on each side than your plywood

1-inch-thick (2.5 cm) foam rubber cut to the same size as the plywood

½-inch (1.3 cm) plywood cut to your desired size

Staple gun with ⅜-inch (.95 cm) staples

Utility knife, craft knife, or scissors

Hammer

Duct tape (optional)

INSTRUCTIONS:

1   Lay the vinyl shiny side down on the table or floor. Center the foam on the vinyl, then place the plywood on the foam. **A**

2   Wrap the sides of vinyl up and around the plywood and staple each side at the center. Pull the vinyl taut and staple every 2 inches (5.1 cm) or so, moving outward and away from the center until you reach all four corners. **B**

3   Working at each corner, pinch the vinyl into a smooth triangle, then fold it over and staple it a few times to secure it. Trim off the excess vinyl and hammer down any staples so no points are protruding. Place duct tape over the stapled area to protect the surface on which you place the board for printing. **C**

4   Flip your printing board and admire the smooth, shiny padded surface just begging you to start printing! **D**

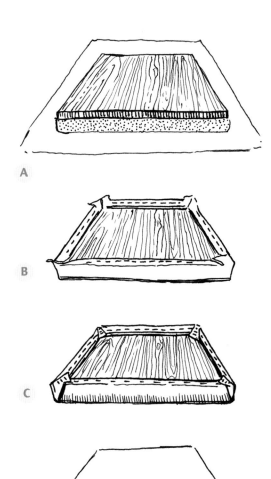

Variation: Build a Print Table

You can always place your print board on an existing table or on a pair of sawhorses, but if you'd like a more stable and permanent fixture for your printing, it's not hard to build your own print table. The whole assembly can be constructed from a few 2 x 4s you can pick up at the home improvement store. Build the print board as directed, but add a structural frame underneath to support the perimeter of the board. Add sturdy legs with locking casters and diagonal braces for stability and support. You'll have lots of room for storage underneath, too! Here are a few factors to consider when designing your print table:

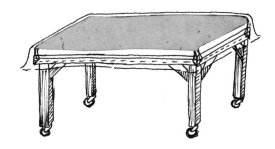

HEIGHT: It should be tall enough so that you don't have to stoop to work, but you should also be able to comfortably reach the center of the table. I'm relatively tall, and my table is 37 inches (.9 m) high, a little taller than a standard kitchen counter.

WIDTH: It should be wide enough to accommodate most common fabrics you will be printing, but not so wide you can't comfortably and effectively place your screen and pull a print in the center area of the table. Mine is 48 inches (1.2 m) wide, ideal for printing most 45-inch-wide (1.1 m) fabric but too narrow for printing 60-inch (1.5 m) fabric,

which I have to slide over to get the full width. Since I use my print table for many purposes besides printing, the optimal work height was more important than going with more width and making it difficult to comfortably reach the center area.

LENGTH: Your print table should be as long as your space will allow. Simply put, the longer the table, the more fabric you can print at once! With this in mind, if you butt multiple sheets of plywood end to end, be sure to reinforce the framework underneath it to support the seams.

PIN FABRIC TO PRINT

Pinning your fabric down to the printing board is remarkably easy, more like staking a tent than pinning pieces together to sew. I recommend starting with a square or rectangular piece of fabric that is smaller than your printing surface. Pinning works the same for any fabric: woven, knit, or felted.

YOU WILL NEED:

Print surface (page 30)

Prewashed fabric

Glass-ball-head pins

INSTRUCTIONS:

1 Lay out your fabric in the center of the board and smooth it with your hands.

2 Push a pin into one corner of the fabric, right near the edge. As you push the pin into the vinyl, angle the point of the pin toward the center of the fabric, just like angling a stake in the ground to keep a tent from blowing away. Be sure the pin is pushed down so the head is flush with the fabric. **A**

3 Pull the side of the fabric taut and pin an adjacent corner, again angling the pin to point toward the center of the fabric. **B**

4 Repeat for the remaining corners of the fabric.

5 Depending on the size of the fabric, you may need to fill in with pins along the sides. I always pin the corners, and then I pin about every 6 to 12 inches (15.2 to 30.5 cm) along each side, making sure the edge is straight and not stretched to severe distortion.

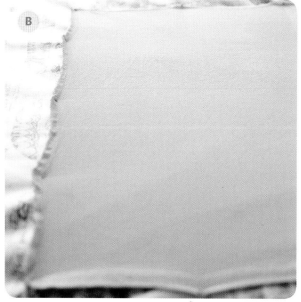

READY, SET, PRINT

Although we'll get into the all-important stencil-making processes in the next couple of chapters, I'd like to introduce you to the mechanics of setting up and printing so you've got a good sense of how it all comes together. Once you've got a stencil on your screen, jump back here to put it to use and pull your first prints!

YOU WILL NEED:

Printing surface: insert, board, or table (pages 29 or 30)

Pins

Prewashed fabric or item to print

Kraft paper (optional)

Clean, dry, and taped screen with stencil

Apron

Gloves (optional)

Spoon

Textile ink

Squeegee

INSTRUCTIONS:

1 Pin your fabric or item to your printing surface and push the pins all the way into the surface so that no pinheads are sticking up. If you are printing a two-sided item like a T-shirt, you can either print it on a T-shirt insert (to conserve space) or slide a piece of kraft paper between the layers.

2 Look through the screen's print window and set the screen on the fabric print side down where you would like the image to print.

3 Spoon a few tablespoons of ink to form a thick bead inside the screen on the reservoir, the taped area just outside the top of the print window, so you can pull the squeegee and ink toward you.

TIPS FOR HAPPY PRINTING

- Keep it neat. Clear away anything on your print table that is not for printing, including setting your coffee somewhere else. A Styrofoam tray from the grocery store makes a great catchall for squeegees, spoons, and ink jars.

- Protect other layers. If you are printing an area of a tee not blocked by an insert (like a sleeve), or other closed form like a pillowcase or a messenger bag, slip a piece of scrap paper behind the print layer to block ink from bleeding through to the other layers of fabric.

- Pin tautly to flatten seams. My friend thought it would be fun to print the backside of her undies, but she didn't pin them taut enough and the ink blobbed up around the seam. We blotted it with a paper towel, and made a note to pin tighter next time!

4 Hold the screen firmly with one hand to keep it from shifting around on the fabric. Use your other hand to grip the squeegee. Starting at the top above the ink, pull the squeegee toward you until you have hit the tape on the other side of the print window. Be sure to put some pressure on the squeegee to push the ink through the screen and down onto the fabric. Repeat if your squeegee is smaller than your design.

5 Carefully lift the screen from the fabric. Congratulations on pulling your first print!

6 Move the screen to the next area you'd like to print and set it down carefully. Or if you are printing tees on an insert, carefully remove the insert, move the tee to another surface or a clothesline to dry, and slide your next tee over the insert. You'll notice it's a little harder to see through the screen with ink on it. For simple prints, it's okay to just eyeball it. Repeat steps 3 and 4 to print the rest of your fabric. If you need to add more ink after a couple prints, spoon it along the top again as you did in step 3. It's better to add a bit of ink as you go than have too much on your screen; it will start to dry in the open air.

CLEANING UP:

When you are finished printing, the first thing to do is wash your screen. Textile paint dries quicker than you'd think, and if it dries on your screen, it can permanently block the screen's holes and inhibit future use. I recommend washing your screen within 20 minutes of printing with textile inks. Rinse your screen with cool water, and if any ink has dried, you can try to spray it out or scrub it with a scrub brush or old toothbrush to knock it loose. Let your screen air-dry or dry it off with a towel.

AIR-DRY AND HEAT-SET YOUR PRINTS:

1 You can let the ink air-dry on the fabric while it is still pinned down to the printing board, or a hair dryer can speed this along if desired. If you need the precious real estate to keep printing, remove the pins, carefully lift the fabric by two corners, and hang it on a line or set it aside to air-dry. Wipe any paint off your vinyl print surface, and your surface is ready to print again!

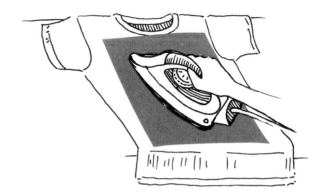

2 Once the ink has air-dried completely, place a piece of clean scrap paper or fabric over the print and iron on the highest setting your fabric will take for a few minutes to heat-set it and make it permanent. Then chuck it into the dryer on high heat for about 15 minutes for good measure. But don't think it's finished and ready to wash after that! Most textile ink manufacturers recommend *curing* the print (letting it set for about a week) before washing.

PULL A
STRIKE-OFF PRINT

Nervous about that first print on your fresh T-shirt or expensive yardage? Or are you unsure just how intense that color you just mixed will look?

Pull a strike-off, or a practice print, on scrap paper. Just lay down a piece of heavy paper that the ink won't soak through—such as kraft paper, freezer paper, or card stock. This way you can see your print before committing to your fabric and make adjustments as needed before printing the real deal.

Once you have printed and reprinted on the strike-off paper a few times, the layered prints make the paper a little piece of art in its own right. Set it aside and then cut it up to make cool little things: note cards, postcards, bookmarks, and end papers for handmade books. Or try using a large roll of newsprint or other cheap paper for your strike-offs. You'll never have to buy wrapping paper again!

CHAPTER 3

LOW-TECH PRINTS

It's time to get down to the nitty-gritty of turning image and pattern design into actual stencils on screens. The stencil concept is simple: anything that blocks the ink from hitting the fabric is a stencil. The array of stencil-making methods, however, is wide-ranging, from improvisational to intricate. Whether you are a spontaneous experimenter open to discovery through happy (and not-so-happy) accidents, or a meticulous planner who prefers to engineer tight, interlocking designs, there is a stencil-making method for you. I'll show you the most immediate and accessible stencil-making techniques first: transferring found textures onto the screen, then cutting stencils and image positives with a craft knife, and finally painting with screen filler and drawing fluid.

BRIEF OVERVIEW

All of the low-tech stencils in this chapter work just fine on fabric with ink right out of the jar—whether you want to use puffy, pearlescent, fluorescent, or even thickened dyes and discharge agents. You can use the chart below to help you find the right technique for your project. Remember to test prints (see Pull a Strike-off Print on page 35) and fine-tune any details of your stencil or placement before jumping into a big project.

	AESTHETIC	ATTRIBUTES	CHALLENGES	PRINT SESSIONS PER STENCIL (APPROXIMATE)
FOUND OBJECT	Textural and imprecise	Direct and documentary	Impermanent, print media gets on original objects	1 to 5
PARAFFIN WAX	Textural and imprecise	Direct and documentary	Stencil gradually wears away as you print	10 to 20
FREEZER PAPER	Crisp and well-defined delineation, intricate cutting	Not limited by screen size, excellent match with thickened dyes	Not durable or reusable	1
CONTACT PAPER	Crisp lines for simple shapes and silhouettes	Can adhere small "island" shapes	Not for fine detail or intricate cutting	10 to 20
ACETATE/MYLAR	Crisp lines for intricate hand cutting	Reusable, can be stored and re-adhered to screen	Avoid small "island" shapes, which are not adhesive and will get lost	10 to 20, more are possible if stencil is reused
SCREEN FILLER ONLY	Direct, painterly and fluid	Immediate and durable; can touch up any other stencil medium	Carefully painting negative background space	20 to 50+
DRAWING FLUID/ SCREEN FILLER	Direct, painterly and fluid	Immediate and durable, can achieve some detail	Allow for drying time of two separate mediums	20 to 50+

TOOLS AND MATERIALS

In this chapter, we'll cover a few different ways to make simple stencils. Depending on the technique you choose, you'll use some, but not all of the materials below. So even though the list looks long, you won't buy all of it! Just read up on the technique that interests you most and come back here to read up on what you need to get started.

SCREEN: All the stencil methods I use also make use of a screen. See page 25 for detailed information on screens and the resource section on page 158 for ordering information.

TAPE: Masking tape is great for patching a leaky stencil or taping paper down to the table to print. And duct tape is my choice for taping screens. It is used to create the print window of the screen and to allow room for an ink reservoir, the starting point for pulling the ink across the stencil. Pick up a big roll at the hardware store, the little one won't be enough. As I mentioned in chapter 2, you need to tape your screen before applying the stencil and prints; see Stretching and Taping Your Screen on page 28.

PARAFFIN WAX: With your screen and a block of paraffin, you can create instant, direct, and true-to-life texture stencils to print with your screen. Available at the grocery store in the canning section, a package of five blocks costs just a couple bucks and lasts for a zillion rubbings. Keep in mind that paraffin wax is soft, so it does not make a permanent stencil. As you print, little bits of the wax are scraped to the side with your squeegee, so at the most you'll get a few dozen prints from the stencil.

FREEZER PAPER: Freezer paper is essentially a lightweight paper that is coated with wax on one side, available in an 18-inch-wide (45.7 cm) roll at the grocery store in the section with sandwich bags and aluminum foil. It is very easy to cut with a craft knife and achieve great detail. Its durability is short-lived, however, since it lasts for only one printing session. This can also be a plus as freezer paper is easy to remove from the fabric after printing. Cutting a freezer paper stencil is so physically easy that you may want to cut through several layers at once; it's as easy as cutting one! For the stencil for the Koi Streamers on page 138, I cut six layers at a time, no problem! Freezer paper is opaque, so if you have a design template, it will go on top of the paper rather than underneath it. You can tape the corners of the template to the freezer paper so it doesn't shift around while you are cutting. Use a photocopy of anything precious that you do not want to cut through and then cut through both layers.

CONTACT PAPER: Not just for prettying up the insides of your mom's kitchen cabinets, peel-and-stick contact paper is terrific for making a quick screen stencil. It is a thin sheet of plastic with backing paper that peels away to expose a sticky back. Pick up a roll at the grocery store or the hardware store. While the paper front is available in clear or different patterns like orange and yellow mushrooms or faux wood grain, the backing paper is often printed with a grid for measuring and cutting. Contact paper is not really reusable, plus it can be tricky to manage when peeling the backing paper off and sticking it to the screen, so I recommend using it for quick and simple stencils. If you are careful when rinsing the ink from your screen, the contact paper will stay adhered to it. For more intricately cut stencils that can be reused, cut them from acetate or Mylar.

ACETATE AND MYLAR: Acetate is a clear plastic sheet used for making copies and transparencies and is available at the office supply store. Mylar is basically a heavier, sturdier version of the same thing available at art- and graphic-supply stores. The nice thing about using either one of these materials as a stencil is that each is washable and reusable, so you can store the stencils off the screen for later use. For the sake of clarity, I am going to refer to the stencil material as acetate; however, the process for cutting and printing with Mylar is exactly the same. I recommend treating the acetate sheet as a solid stencil; you may cut out "windows" but avoid cutting little "island" pieces that must be adhered onto the screen with a glue stick. They're elusive bits of ephemera to keep track of in your stencil file, and they also can accidentally disappear down the drain while rinsing the screen, especially since glue sticks are water soluble. For detailed stencils with small island pieces, I recommend using photo emulsion (see Chapter 4).

Since acetate is transparent, you can place an image underneath it for tracing. The easiest way to transfer and cut your image is to do it all at once. Just tape the image to your cutting mat, tape the acetate on top of it, and cut the acetate. If you have an original image that you want to preserve or use again, follow the same process but trace it on the acetate with permanent marker, remove it, and then cut the acetate. Or you can photocopy your original and use the copy for the transfer.

CRAFT KNIFE: You could cut stencils with scissors for large areas, but this is not easy if you are going for detail. For fine precision work, use a craft knife with a fresh blade. Hold the knife like a pencil when cutting on a mat. Change your blades often—I'm talking about every 15 to 30 minutes of use. Seriously, I buy blades in packs of 100. A dull blade is more dangerous than a sharp one because it is far more likely to catch and slip. This loss of control can inflict mistakes and injuries. When I toss a blade out, I always stick a piece of tape around its edge before discarding it as a safety precaution. You don't want it to slice the trash bag or the person carrying it.

SELF-HEALING CUTTING MAT: Get the most mileage out of your blades (and save your work surfaces) by cutting on a cutting mat. Make sure your mat is larger than your project so your hand and knife are not slipping off the side. And if you work on your lap instead of a table, place a board or old book larger than your mat underneath it, between the knife and your leg. I still remember a fellow student in art class who stabbed himself in the thigh with his craft knife. You don't want to be like that guy, standing there in his boxer shorts with his jeans around his knees while the professor rummaged through the first aid kit to get him a bandage.

SCREEN FILLER: Screen filler is exactly what it sounds like. It's a red, water-soluble liquid stencil applied to the screen to fill the holes, and when it dries, it becomes waterproof and blocks ink from passing through. Comparable to photo emulsion in its durability, screen filler can withstand many printings and washings for months. Essentially, you are painting the areas to be blocked out.

To use screen filler by itself, simply paint it on the dry, clean screen with a brush. Let it air dry completely (usually a couple of hours) and be sure to keep the screen surface elevated but level so gravity does not cause the filler to run. Once it is dry, it is ready to print.

DRAWING FLUID: Drawing fluid is used only in conjunction with screen filler. When considering whether to use screen filler by itself or drawing fluid, I look at what would be the most efficient: will it be quicker and easier to paint the image itself or the area around it? It just depends on the design. Drawing fluid is applied to the screen first and acts as a resist to the screen filler. With drawing fluid, you are painting the positive areas (the areas that will print), and resisting the screen filler to create the stencil. Then squeegee the screen filler over it to create the background and details.

FOUND-TEXTURE STENCILS

Start looking around the room, or venture out into the world, in search of great textures. Textures that are optimal for wax rubbings have a relatively flat, two-dimensional plane against which you can place your screen and have a well-defined texture—so nothing too subtle. Gravestones, manhole covers, stove burners, and license plates are good examples. But you will find so many more once you start looking around. If you start with a composition of small, found objects, arrange them on a hard surface such as a table or countertop and then make your wax stencil just like you would any found texture.

This is a good process to use with your rougher, dingier, less pristine screens. If it's got a little ink or clogged holes, it will work fine for wax rubbings.

YOU WILL NEED:

Clean, dry, and taped screen

A textured object or surface

1 block of paraffin wax

Printing surface: insert, board, or table

Pins

Prewashed fabric or item to print

Apron

Gloves (optional)

Spoon

Textile ink

Squeegee

Iron and ironing surface

Scrap paper, newspaper, newsprint, or brown kraft paper

INSTRUCTIONS:

1   Place the screen with the print side flat against the textured object. Hold it firmly with one hand to keep it from shifting around.

2   Rub the block of paraffin vigorously against the squeegee side of the screen directly over the object to pick up its texture. This will create a negative impression: where you pick up the texture in the wax, the holes will be blocked and the empty space will print. Keep in mind that the entire print window shape is still open, so you will print a rectangle or square print window, resisted with some textures. **A**

3 Print as usual. For a refresher, check out page 33.

4 Use *cold* water to rinse the ink off your screen after each print session; hot water will melt the stencil right out! Over several print sessions, you'll notice the paraffin-wax stencil wearing out, becoming more faint and less resistant to the ink being printed through it. You can even see little bits of wax accumulate on your squeegee as you drag it across the screen. Once it has worn too far, you can re-rub your texture or reclaim the wax from the screen and start with something else.

To reclaim the paraffin wax from a screen, it must be melted out. You can spray the screen with very hot tap water; if that doesn't work, just iron it out of the screen between some scrap paper, which I've found to be a more reliable and complete reclamation method. Place a few sheets of scrap paper (I use old newspaper or brown kraft paper) on your ironing board, place the waxy screen face down, and layer a few more sheets on top. Set the iron to medium heat and iron the stack. It will melt the wax off the screen and onto the scrap paper. Be sure not to iron on the taped areas of the screen and to keep the iron moving so it doesn't burn the screen mesh. You can use the point of the iron to get into the corners of the print window. Change out the scrap paper as it becomes saturated, and hold the screen up to the light to check for any wax you missed. Discard the waxy scrap paper, and your screen is ready for its next image!

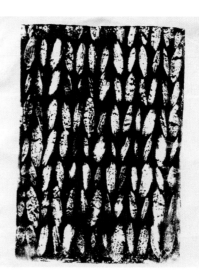

TIP

To create a simple shaped stencil with texture, say of a fleur-de-lis motif, cut it out of contact paper or acetate and apply it to the print side of the wax-textured screen. For an opposite effect, place the fleur-de-lis motif itself in the center of the print window; this will create a textured field the size and shape of the print window with a motif showing on the unprinted fabric from underneath.

RADIATOR GRILL STENCILS

While traveling in Europe in the spring of 2003, my husband, Paul, and I wandered into a tiny clothing shop in Barcelona, Spain. It was run by a young woman who worked alone, sewing and printing behind a curtain in the back of the shop and displaying her original creations in the front of the shop. I purchased an asymmetric, sleeveless white shirt with a black geometric pattern printed on it. Looking around, I noticed the pattern on the shirt had probably been printed from the grill of the little radiator heating her shop. I could even see layers of black paint that had built up on the radiator's surface—probably from repeated printing! I think she was inking up the radiator, laying the fabric on it, and pressing the fabric to pick up the print. Unfortunately, the language barrier between her Catalan and my English hindered my ability to share my excitement with her. But I loved seeing the incorporation of the textures around her into her work.

CONTACT PAPER STENCILS

I love the immediacy of contact paper, also known as self-adhesive shelf liner. From it, you can quickly cut simple shapes in mere seconds, peel the paper backing to expose the sticky back, and apply it to the screen. By itself, contact paper's effect is bold and graphic, but in conjunction with other techniques, it's even better, from creating a textured motif with paraffin wax rubbing (see my Honeycomb Folding Screen on page 120) to making a solid silhouette layer to print with a finely detailed image (see Tough Guy Baby Jumpers on page 132).

YOU WILL NEED:

Fine-point marker, pen, or pencil

Sheet of contact paper slightly larger than
  your print window

Craft knife

Cutting mat

Clean, dry, taped screen

Tape (optional)

INSTRUCTIONS:

1 Draw your design on the gridded backing paper side of the contact paper and mark an X on any areas you plan to cut out; these windows will be the areas that print. Remember that your image should be smaller than the print window, and what your image looks like on the sticky side (the gridded backing paper side) is the orientation that it will print. Using the craft knife on the cutting mat, cut your image stencil out of the contact paper.

2 Make sure your cut areas fall within the print window and that the paper overlaps the edge of the print window. Remove the backing and apply the stencil to the print side of the screen. Be sure your image is centered within the print window; if any overlaps onto the taped borders, it won't print.

Smooth down the contact paper, making sure the stencil edges adhere to the screen. If there are any open areas between the edges of the contact paper and the outside of the print window, fill in with masking tape or scrap contact paper as needed.

3 *Wow, that was quick!* You now have a screen that is ready to print. For a refresher on printing, jump back to page 33.

ACETATE STENCILS

By cutting stencils from acetate, you can create a crisp, detailed stencil, tape it to your screen, and print with it in minutes. Its transparency lends well to tracing; it's excellent for cutting graphic imagery and text. Since acetate is not adhesive, just cut out the areas you want to print and you won't have to keep track of little island pieces that don't stick to the screen. When I'm done printing with an acetate stencil, I carefully remove it from the screen, wash and dry it, and keep it in a file for reuse in future print sessions.

YOU WILL NEED:

Fine-point marker, pen, or pencil

Sheet of acetate slightly larger than your print window

Craft knife

Cutting mat

Clean, dry, and taped screen

Semipermanent tape, such as blue painter's tape
   or masking tape

INSTRUCTIONS:

1   Draw your design on the acetate and mark any areas you plan to cut out with an X; these windows will be the areas that print. Using the craft knife on the cutting mat, cut out your image stencil. Remember that it should be smaller than your print window.

2   Place the screen print side up on your work surface. Place the acetate stencil on the print side (outside) of the screen, centering it over the print window. When you look at the screen from the print side, it will be backward—so when you flip it over to the squeegee side down to print, it will be oriented the right way for printing.

3   Completely tape the perimeter of the stencil to the screen so that when you print, no ink seeps through any gaps between the stencil and screen onto the fabric. You now have a screen that is ready to print! For a refresher on printing, jump back to page 33.

4   To remove the acetate stencil after printing, simply peel off the tape, carefully lift the stencil, and clean any ink off of the stencil and the screen. If it is still in good shape after lots of printing sessions, simply store it in a file and then tape it back on a screen to print with it again.

FREEZER-PAPER STENCILS

Freezer paper is a bit of a departure from the other hand-cut screen stencils like contact paper and acetate. With the others, you start with the sheet of stencil materials, cut out windows to print, and attach the stencil to the screen. We'll still cut out the print areas from freezer paper, but instead of attaching the paper to the screen, we'll iron it directly on the prewashed fabric to be printed. Then you are not limited by the screen size and you can create much larger stencils. Since freezer paper is basically white butcher paper with a thin plastic coating on one side, it is very easy to slice through multiple layers at once.

YOU WILL NEED:

Freezer paper

Masking tape or Scotch tape

Cutting mat

Fine-point marker, pen, or pencil

Craft knife

Iron and hard ironing surface, like a worktable

Prewashed fabric

INSTRUCTIONS:

1   Cut and stack as many layers of freezer paper with the shiny side down as you would like to cut at once. If you want to mirror the image on any layers, flip those so the shiny side is up. Tape all layers together at the corners so they don't shift while you are cutting and place the stack on the cutting mat.

2   Draw your design on the stencil and mark an X in the areas that print. Cut them all out with the craft knife.

3   Iron the fabric you plan to print so it is wrinkle-free. Then place the freezer-paper stencil shiny side down on the fabric and iron it in place. Set the iron at medium setting and keep it moving around the stencil. It only takes a few seconds for the iron to melt the waxy side of the paper and adhere it to the fabric to sufficiently to block any colorant from the fabric.

4   Since the stencil is on the fabric and not the screen, you can apply the colorant directly to the fabric a few different ways. Whichever one you use, have some fun and experiment with mixing and blending different colors on the exposed fabric areas while they are blocked by the paper stencil. Just be careful to keep the layers of color thin so they don't create a crunchy, raised surface; after all, the fabric ought to retain its pliable properties! Remember, if you are working on a closed item like a tee or a pillowcase, work on a T-shirt insert or slide a piece of scrap paper between the layers to block the colorant from bleeding onto the second side of fabric.

Here are some techniques to try:

- Paint ink with a brush.

- Use a squeegee to print ink through a blank screen or a paraffin wax-textured screen for a little added pattern variation.

- Squeegee thickened dye or discharge agent with a decal spreader (jump ahead to Beyond Ink on page 86).

5 Once your freshly colored areas are dry, peel the freezer paper off the fabric and heat-set the ink (page 35). For dye or discharge agents, follow the instructions on page 103 to cure, steam, and wash your fabric.

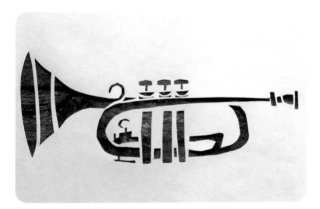

STENCILS ON THE GO

I travel a lot for my business, selling my handmade wares out of a tent at all sorts of art fairs. Luckily, I found I can cut stencils no matter my location thanks to a little 9 x 12-inch (22.9 x 30.5 cm) cutting mat that I take on the road with me. Since my booth space is limited, I usually work on my lap, but I always use an old book to support the cutting mat. I also cut a few pieces of stencil material the size of the print windows of my screens ahead of time. I pack them by placing them in the book along with my cutting mat. Then as long as I've got my craft knife and a pack of blades, I am ready to go.

DRAWING-FLUID AND SCREEN-FILLER STENCILS

Perhaps you would rather paint your stencils than cut them. Painted stencils can be handy for text, but remember, if you are working from the print side of the screen you'll need to reverse your lettering. If you have trouble thinking in reverse, you can work from the front/the squeegee side instead. But in order to keep the screen elevated so the drawing fluid/screen filler doesn't spread to the work surface, you need to jack it up from the table. You can use a similar-size screen and lay it squeegee side up on the table, then set the screen you are painting on top of it, also squeegee side up. Then you can paint from the front of the screen and you don't have to try to flip the text or image in your mind. To use screen filler on its own, simply paint the stencil areas—the ones you don't want to print—and let it dry. To work with drawing fluid, it takes a few more steps, though it can make things go more quickly. It just depends on the level of detail and amount of screen you need to fill.

YOU WILL NEED:

Paintbrush for painting your detailed design

Drawing fluid

Clean, dry, and taped screen

Squeegee

Screen filler

Sink with a spray hose

Towel for drying the screen

INSTRUCTIONS:

1   Paint drawing fluid on the screen. Make sure it is applied thickly enough to penetrate through the holes of the screen and does not just sit on top of the mesh. Remember, wherever you paint the drawing fluid, ink will eventually come through the screen, so you're drawing the design you want to print. **A**

2   Allow the drawing fluid to dry completely; this means that it should not feel tacky or sticky to the touch. I do not recommend using a blow dryer to speed things along: you'll end up with a dry skin on the fluid, with liquid fluid underneath that takes even longer to dry. Just let it air dry on its own for a couple of hours.

3   Squeegee a smooth, even layer of screen filler on the same side of the screen as you applied the drawing fluid. You will notice the blue drawing fluid resist the red screen filler. **B**

4 Allow the screen filler to dry completely; it should take a couple of hours.

5 Spray out the drawing fluid with room-temperature to cool water. It's water soluble and will rinse out of the mesh, leaving the screen filler intact.

6 Simply wipe the water off your screen with a towel and you're ready to print!

RECLAIMING SCREEN FILLER FROM A SCREEN

When you're good and done with the stencil on your screen and never want to print it again, it's time to reclaim it, to clean the stencil off the screen so you can start over with something new. The screen filler liquid should tell you what to use right on the jar: usually it's as simple as "Use Greased Lightning." (For the uninitiated, Greased Lightning is a particular brand of household cleaner available at the grocery store or hardware store.) Spray it on the screen, let it sit a few minutes to dissolve the screen filler, scrub it out with a nylon scrub brush, and rinse with water. Your screen is now ready for its next printing adventure!

CHAPTER 4

DETAILED PRINTS

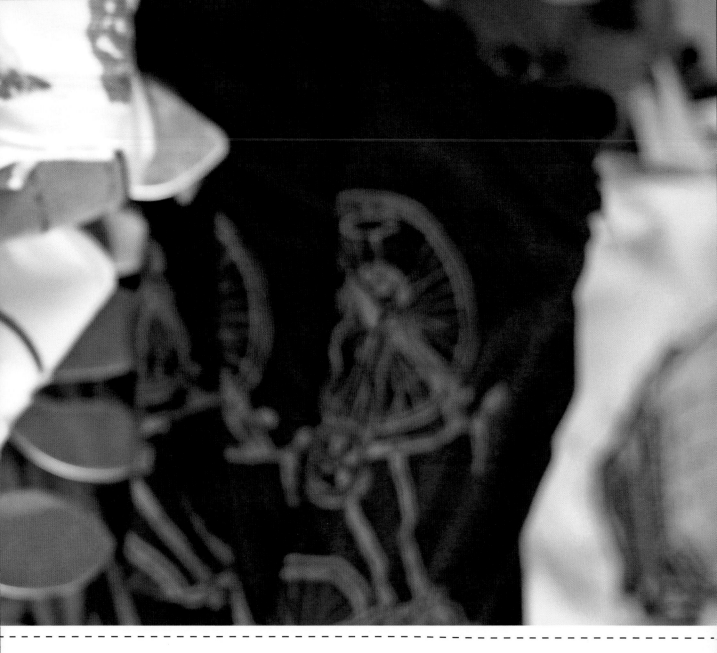

By now, I'm sure you're itching to understand how to print finely detailed drawings, photography, and text. I was lured to more detailed stencil techniques to harvest imagery from years of sketchbooks and several continents of travel journals. Sushi for breakfast in Japan, the Giudecca Canal in Venice, the Cockspur Beacon lighthouse off Tybee Island in Georgia—all these prints have started as little sketches and made for amazing imagery on Jennythreads apparel.

In this chapter you'll learn how to fine-tune your imagery as well as process it with photo emulsion to make a durable, professional-grade screen that prints beautifully for months. The process takes some trial and error, so it can seem daunting at first. But I am happy to report that with a little experience, it is also gratifying!

TOOLS AND MATERIALS

The key to making finely detailed stencils is developing clean, crisp, and communicative artwork. This often involves a trip to the copy shop and a little photo editing, either on the computer or the good old-fashioned way with a black marker and a craft knife (I work back and forth between the two). You'll be able to take a ho-hum photo and transform it into a crisp and clear screen image to print on your fabric.

COMPUTER WITH PHOTO-EDITING SOFTWARE: With the availability of copyright-free imagery online, it can be very convenient to download an image to manipulate and print as well as use your own original imagery. You don't need fancy software, and for our purposes of transforming an image into a screen stencil, you can do it with the basic software that came with your computer, and even on your phone, as long as you can print the image when you're done editing it. For my favorite photo-editing tricks, check out page 58.

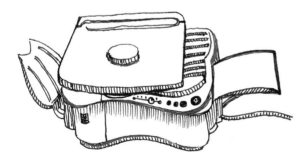

LASER COPIER OR COPY SHOP: You can print out your images with an ink-jet printer, but when it is time to make transparencies for photo emulsion, you will need to have

your images laser-copied onto acetate to make transparencies. Laser copiers use carbon-based toner, which is more dense and opaque than the ink that comes out of ink-jet printers. If you are just trying out photo emulsion and need only a few copies, you can run to the copy shop, but if your production level increases, you may want to buy a basic copier of your own.

TRANSPARENCY ON OTHER IMAGE POSITIVE: To make a transparency, I recommend making two identical black and white laser copies of your image on acetate, sandwiching them together, and affixing the transparency sandwich with a little Scotch tape. This way, in the process of exposing your emulsion-coated screen to light, the opaque image will block the light and eventually become the crisp, finely detailed stencil through which you print. You can also use black construction paper to make an image positive (see page 60).

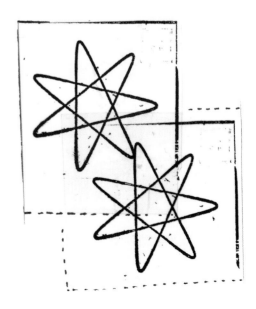

SCOTCH TAPE: Fresh from the desk is Scotch tape, a necessity for keeping transparencies in place, whether they are sandwiched together (as they should be) or arranged in the exposure unit to fit within the screen's print window. Since Scotch tape is completely transparent, it won't inadvertently make tape-shaped print areas on your screen.

PHOTO EMULSION: Photo emulsion is a film that hardens into a durable stencil when exposed to light. You will use an emulsion scoop to coat it on your screen in a darkroom and then shoot it with your image transparency in a light-exposure unit. Due to its short shelf life once it is mixed (a few weeks to a couple months), I recommend purchasing a quart at a time versus buying in bulk and getting a gallon. I have yet to use up even a quart when coating a dozen or more large screens. And then I drive my husband Paul crazy by keeping the leftover emulsion in our home fridge for months at a time, never getting around to my next batch of screens before it's gone bad.

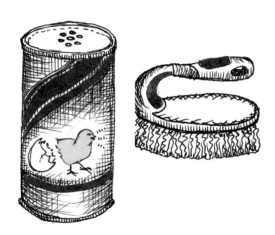

SCRUB BRUSH AND DEGREASER: To prepare your screen for coating with photo emulsion, you need to remove any dirt, oils, or other chemicals that could interfere with the emulsion adhering properly to your screen mesh. A general-purpose scrub brush and good old Bon Ami, Comet, or Ajax (all mild abrasives in the household cleaning section of the grocery store) are all you need for this stage of the game.

NOTE   A recent innovation is the development of photo emulsion sheets with acetate backing, which I really like. They don't make the mess of coating the screen as liquid emulsion does. Follow the manufacturer's directions; they're pretty simple. Here's the gist of it: wet your screen with a spritz of water, apply the sheet of emulsion to the screen and squeegee both sides. Then let it dry completely, peel off the plastic backing, and shoot your screen. All other rules of working with photo emulsion still apply: you still need to work in a darkroom and do test swatches to figure the exposure time, and the sheets have the same short shelf life. Also, in my experience with emulsion sheets, when I peel the acetate backing, it pulls off some of the emulsion at the edges of the print window. I usually fill in the gaps with a little tape or screen filler.

EMULSION SCOOP: An emulsion scoop is an elongated metal trough that contains and directs liquid emulsion onto your screen smoothly, evenly, and neatly. I recommend getting an emulsion scoop that is about the width of your print window; it should definitely fit inside your screen frame. It is possible to coat emulsion with a squeegee, but it takes a lot more control—meaning lots of practice—and even then, it's still pretty messy. If you decide to go with photo emulsion sheets instead of the liquid, you won't need the scoop.

In graduate school, we had a large exposure table with a vacuum that sucked a flexible rubber lid down over the screen to ensure good contact with the image. I could just flip one switch to turn on the vacuum and another for the lights. This type of light table is terrific but expensive and large—impractical for a home studio or even a small studio. In the opposite direction, in my first apartment after graduate school, I really improvised! I don't recommend this method because it is slow and the light is uneven and difficult to calibrate, but it can be done: I used a photo floodlight bulb in a clip light on the leg of my ironing board. Then, several years later, after almost drop-kicking the clip-light apparatus across my driveway in tearful frustration, I spent some money and got a basic four-bulb black-light exposure unit. It's my happy medium between the rigged-up, clip-light jalopy and a vacuum-sealed behemoth like the one in graduate school. I still have to do a little rigging to weigh the screens, but at least I can get consistent exposure times. To set up your own at-home exposure unit, check out page 62.

EXPOSURE UNIT: Since photo emulsion is developed by light, you need a light source. The sun is too powerful and unpredictable a light source for this process, so you need an exposure unit you can control. I tried exposing screens outside on a sunny afternoon once and watched the green emulsion burn right to a scary charred brown, skipping blue—the desired color—and hardness completely!

DIGITAL TIMER: More sophisticated than the basic egg timer and its tiny marks to show minutes, a digital kitchen timer is essential for calibrating your screen exposure times and getting consistent results so you don't have to reclaim and recoat screens (trust me, you'll want to get it right!). Make sure it can measure minutes and seconds. You can pick one up in the kitchen section of the grocery store or department store.

SCREEN: That's right, you'll need to get out your screen. See page 25 for detailed information on screens and the resource section on page 158 for ordering information.

SPRAY NOZZLE OR PRESSURE WASHER: You'll need to use a high-pressure spray nozzle to spray out your screens; the wimpy one on your kitchen sink does not provide enough pressure to clear out the emulsion efficiently. I got a spray nozzle and 6-foot (1.8 m) hose that I rigged up to the water connection to my studio washing machine. A garden spray nozzle that attaches to a garden hose works very well, too. Don't have a spigot and nozzle to fit it? Wrap your exposed screen in a black trash bag or dark towels to keep sunlight out and spray it out at the car wash!

SCREEN RECLAIMER AND SPRAY BOTTLE: When you purchase your photo emulsion, it is also a good idea to get a bottle of screen reclaimer, a solvent made specifically for dissolving old emulsion out of your screen. It is sold in a concentrate that must be diluted with water, so I recommend getting a spray bottle to mix it into also.

CUSTOM-MADE SCREENS AND STENCILS

If you read through this chapter and decide you're not all that interested in tackling the trial and error challenge of photo emulsion, you still have options. There are plenty of businesses online, and maybe even in your town, that have the equipment and willingness to make custom screens with which you can print. That said, I recommend that you review this chapter to better understand the processes so you can prepare your imagery to its advantage. I hated to study weaving and especially computer-aided jacquard design, and I never got the hang of knitting. But at least these experiences helped me understand fabric structures, knowledge that is very useful when ordering fabric and designing apparel since that is how I make my living.

The Darkroom

Sure it's not technically a tool or material, but it is a necessity for working with photo emulsion. Don't let that scare you away! I have always made do with a windowless room like a bathroom or closet. The space needs to be large enough to coat and maneuver one screen at a time, as well as store all screens horizontally and undisturbed until they are completely dry (usually overnight). Figure out where each screen will go to dry so you are not rearranging things in the dark while juggling screens and squeegees wet with emulsion. Photo emulsion is goopy and messy; it also dries hard and leaves stains. So cover your work surface with plastic sheeting or an old towel before starting. Wear an apron and rubber gloves, too. Emulsion develops and hardens with light, but this happens in a couple minutes, not in fractions of seconds like photography film. It is fine to work with the door cracked for a little bit of light, or you can pick up a red safety lightbulb to illuminate your darkroom from a photo supply store.

Set up a place in your darkroom for the exposure unit as well, and think about how you will shelter the other screens from the light as you expose each screen. I use my studio bathroom, clear off a wire shelving unit, and cover the side that is most exposed to direct light with dark fabric, cardboard, or anything to keep the light out. When I am done coating all the screens, I even tape over the cracks around the door to block all light from the room. Once the screens are completely dry to the touch, it is fine to stack them in a corner and cover the stack with the dark material.

GETTING ORGANIZED FOR THE DARKROOM

Are you planning to shoot multiple screens? Before cleaning and coating, lay out all imagery on the blank screens to be sure they fit and make adjustments as needed. Number each screen, write it on the screen with a marker, name the imagery, and then make a numbered list of screens and corresponding imagery while you are still working in a lit area. Once you are in the darkroom shooting screens, use the list to determine which image goes on each screen; this speeds the exposure process immensely. Similarly, if you have to weight your screens down with bricks or books to maintain consistent contact between the transparency and the screen for a crisp, clear image, find ones that fit before coating your screens so you are not scrambling in the darkroom.

EDITING AND MANIPULATING YOUR IMAGES

Turning your source material into print-ready images can be as easy or involved as you want it to be. I often use a permanent marker and craft knife for simple outlines. However, I use the computer to take care of some basic picture issues that I can't do so easily by hand, such as printing an image out of my phone. On the following pages, I'll go through the process for both.

EDITING AN IMAGE BY HAND:

1 To doctor an image manually, I use a fat black permanent marker, a fine-point pen, and a craft knife. I use the craft knife as an eraser to cleanly and precisely cut away unwanted details and blemishes, fuzzy and blurry areas, and to separate the image from its background. If you need to get a sense of how your image will print, just make a black-and-white photocopy of it. This helps to flatten out the variations in the image and to reduce or increase the image size.

2 Making a photocopy of the photocopy if you want to will also increase the contrast, though each successive copy will be lower quality, and you could lose some fine detail. Be sure the copier is set to the darkest setting to produce a rich, saturated black.

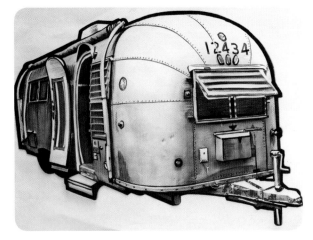

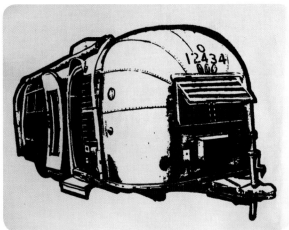

For this Airstream image, I copied my original photo and used a marker to outline the areas I wanted to print. Then I used a craft knife to remove the areas I didn't want to print.

EDITING AN IMAGE WITH A COMPUTER:

1   Crop out background and unnecessary space and information so your image takes up the whole page. This isolates the image, making it more singular and graphically powerful. If you want to use any cutting tools such as the Polygonal Lasso or the Magic Wand Tool to isolate your image here, feel free. Or when you print it out, you can cut it out with a craft knife.

2   Resize the image in the software program; the nice thing is that you can be very precise. It's a lot easier to get the exact image size you need this way; it sure beats putting your image on a copier and guessing the percentage to enlarge or reduce it. This is also an option when printing: you can modify the page layout and sizing within the printing preview window.

3   Change the image mode from color to grayscale or black and white. Don't convert it to a text file—you will lose a whole lot of detail. In some programs, this can be found in the Effects menu.

4   Get rid of midtone grays. Increase brightness and contrast to get rid of a lot of the middle tones and achieve a more starkly graphic, black-and-white image. Also, try playing with adjusting shadows, midtones, and highlights. I find when I lighten the shadows, a lot more detail shows up that was lost in the dark before.

5   Retouch and clean up flaws, blemishes, unwanted details, and distractions with just a few retouching clicks. To me, this is the real magic of photo editing. What wrinkles? What scratches? I don't see anything but smooth perfection.

6   Print the image. I recommend that before you print, you preview the image so you can have a good look at it. If necessary, fine-tune the print size before committing it to paper. Be sure to orient the image correctly to best fill the page. For example, my Airstream camper (on the previous page) is oriented horizontally so I choose Landscape. If I were printing my lonely robot (at right), I would choose Portrait orientation. If you don't, the program could automatically set it to the default setting, and the Airstream would be printed with its length running the shorter dimension of the printed page, not an efficient format at all.

Here's an example of a low-contrast photo that I processed with the computer and turned into a high-contrast print.

7 Even when I use the computer to edit an image, I still work back into it with pen and knife. I often add more detail with a marker and cut out unwanted fuzzy areas with the craft knife.

8 Enlarge the artwork if you need to. What if you want to print out an image that is much larger than a sheet of copy paper? I do not recommend trying to tile an image from a bunch of sections printed out on your computer. There are easier and less frustrating ways. If you just need to enlarge an image once in a while, send the file to a local copy shop and have them print it out in the desired size. Or trace it onto a large sheet of paper or acetate with an art projector.

9 Now it is time to make a transparency. To prepare your image to make a photo emulsion stencil on a screen, you must print your imagery on a transparency. The goal is for the image to block the light while the transparent acetate it is copied onto does not. Remember, the image is a positive; what is black is what will print.

Using the laser copier or copy shop, copy the imagery onto two sheets of acetate. One copy is usually not opaque enough to block light from your emulsion, so you must use two. Just hit the Copy button two times in a row before removing your original from the copy machine. Cut excess areas of acetate away from the imagery. Line up the two layers of the imagery as exactly as possible, one sheet on top of the other, and then tape them together with transparent tape.

DESIGN A SILHOUETTE LAYER

If you really want to add some dimension to a detailed screen image, make a second screen that works as a fill layer (in other words, a silhouette that colors the image from behind). I guarantee that your two-toned design will leap right off the fabric. This is so cool and surprisingly easy—I use it for a lot of T-shirts that I sell. For instructions, see the Tough Guy Baby Jumpers on page 132.

CONSTRUCTION-PAPER STENCILS

Oftentimes when I want to make an image positive, I don't use a photograph as a starting point at all. Instead, I'll use black construction paper and a craft knife to create a design. I love it partly because it is challenging, meditative, and it progresses organically. On the practical side, it is a dry process and is very portable. Remember, the image is a positive; what is black is what will print.

YOU WILL NEED:

Black construction paper

Pen or pencil for sketching your preliminary design

Craft knife

Cutting mat

Scotch tape for fixing mistakes

Softcover book or folder to carry your paper
  cutting kit

INSTRUCTIONS:

1   Precut the black construction paper to fit within the print window of your screen. It can be a freeform shape or a repeat module shape.

2   You can either draw your design on the paper and then cut around it or just go for it and start cutting! To keep yourself from getting confused, you can mark an X on the areas to be cut away. Then, carefully cut away the areas you don't want to print. It's up to you how bold or detailed you want to cut.

3   If you make any mistakes and cut off something important, just tape it back on with a little Scotch tape. Be sure to cut any excess tape sticking out so it doesn't become an unsightly stencil itself.

4   Store your cut-paper design flat in a book or folder until you are ready use it to make your screen. Your paper positive is ready for photo emulsion processing.

COATING YOUR SCREEN

Ready to use those image positives you just made? Good news! Coating your screen with emulsion is the first step to making them into wonderful, printable stencil imagery. You've got a jar of photo emulsion and a few screens, but the emulsion won't climb out of the jar onto the screen itself—so you've got to coat it on the screen. You will pour the emulsion into a scoop, hold the screen vertically, and drag it across both the print side and squeegee side of the screen mesh to coat them evenly. And you'll be doing this in a darkroom with very little light, so it's a good idea to read the instructions first!

 I highly recommend making your test swatches when you are coating your screens (see Calibrating Exposure Time with Test Swatches on page 64).

YOU WILL NEED:

Work surface

Photo emulsion and developer

Emulsion scoop, slightly wider than the print window but still within screen-frame size

Stretched, taped, and degreased screen

Drying area

Fan

INSTRUCTIONS:

1 Mix the developer into the photo emulsion if you haven't already. Pour the photo emulsion into the trough of the scoop.

2 Stand the screen on the work surface and hold it vertically at the top. Hold the scoop at the bottom edge of the print window on the print side of the screen.

3 Tip the screen back so that the line of emulsion in the scoop is making contact with the screen.

4 Smoothly pull the scoop up, coating the entire print window, then stop. **A**

5 Tip the screen forward to let any excess emulsion run back into the scoop.

6 Pull the scoop up and away from the print window.

7 Flip the screen and repeat on the inside of the screen. What you want is a smooth, even coat on both sides of the screen, thick enough to cover the print window but not so thick that it drips or runs. It is okay to use the scoop to scrape excess emulsion and smooth out the coat before letting it dry.

8 Place the screen horizontally in your darkroom drying area. If, after you let the screen dry, you see lots of drips, wash it off and recoat it. The drips will interfere with your image, and it is not worth trying to expose a gloppy screen—it will only lead to more frustration.

A

EXPOSING YOUR SCREEN

My instructions here are for using a rigged-up exposure unit with a photoflood bulb in which the light source shines from above the screen. **A** If you're using a unit where the light source shines from below the glass, the only change you'll need to make when setting up is that the transparency goes down on the glass first, then the screen (print side down), then the books to weight it. **B** Whatever unit you use, be sure to calibrate the exposure time with test swatches (see page 64) before shooting your screens.

A

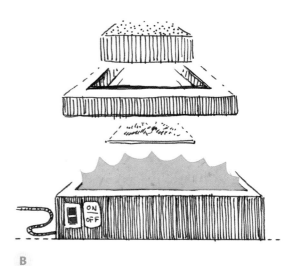

B

YOU WILL NEED:

A book or box, slightly thicker than the screen frame, to fit inside the print window of the screen (figure out which books will fit within each screen before coating it)

Screen, coated with photo emulsion and dried

Image positive transparency or imagery cut from black construction paper

¼-inch (.6 cm) (or thicker) pane of glass, larger than the print window

Utility knife blade or razor blade

Light exposure unit

Digital timer that shows minutes and seconds

Spray nozzle attached to a spigot or faucet

INSTRUCTIONS:

1 Place the book on the floor or table.

2 Place the emulsion-coated screen on top of it, print side facing up.

3 Place your transparencies on the screen, then a piece of glass bigger than the print window to ensure good contact.

4 Use the blade to scrape any dust or debris from the glass that could block light from the screen.

5 Turn on the light, start the timer, and expose the screen according to your test swatch.

6 When the timer beeps, turn off the light and remove the screen.

7 Spray out the screen with the spray nozzle. It takes a couple of minutes for the emulsion to soften before it starts washing out. Keep at it until your design is clear. A

8 Place your exposed screen in a bright area to let the emulsion dry out and firm up. I usually let it harden overnight before printing a freshly exposed screen.

Excellent! Your finely detailed, durable, and strong emulsion-stenciled screen is ready for months of printing. Enjoy it, you deserve it! Jump back to page 33 to put it to use.

A freshly exposed and sprayed screen.

A

CALIBRATING EXPOSURE TIME WITH TEST SWATCHES

So just how long should you expose your screen? It varies considerably, depending on the brand of emulsion and each light source. You need to figure it out for yourself with your own test swatches. Photo emulsion has a short shelf life, and these swatches will change and become inaccurate over time, so I recommend making a set of test swatches with each new batch of screens as you coat them. I use a finely detailed image transparency to give me a small margin of error and the most precision in timing. At first it seems vague, but as you expose and study your swatches, you will be able to fine-tune it. Trust me, it is a whole lot easier to wash swatches than to reclaim and recoat screens!

YOU WILL NEED:

12 x 12-inch (30.5 x 30.5 cm) square piece of mesh

12 x 12-inch (30.5 x 30.5 cm) frame, which can be made from stretcher strips

Staple gun and staples

Photo emulsion

Craft knife or utility knife

Scissors

Image transparency with fine lines and details

Light exposure unit

A book or box, for a weight

Digital timer that shows minutes and seconds

Cold water from a faucet or spray nozzle

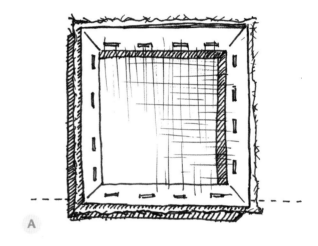

A

INSTRUCTIONS:

1   Stretch a 12-inch (30.5 cm) square piece of mesh to a small frame as shown, such as one snapped together from 12-inch (30.5 cm) stretcher strips. A For a refresher, see Stretch Your Screen on page 28, though you won't need to bother taping this screen. Coat the screen on both sides with emulsion (see page 61) and set it aside to dry. B

2   When the screen is dry, use a craft knife to cut out the coated mesh. C Then use scissors to cut the mesh into 3-inch (7.6 cm) squares; this yields 16 test swatches. D Keep the swatches in a dark place with your coated screens. You will use these to calibrate the exposure time for this batch of screens.

B

At this point you should read any directions, charts, or literature about your particular exposure unit that could give you a clue of a starting exposure time. The same screen coated with the same emulsion could take 2 minutes in a large vacuum-sealed exposure table, 7 minutes in a black-light four-bulb unit, and it could take half an hour or more under a floodlight clipped to a table leg.

3 Each test swatch is like a miniature screen that you will shoot one at a time. Place your transparency on the glass, top with the test swatch, and weight it down. Set your timer at your researched time or at 5 minutes (see above). Start your timer and turn your exposure light on at the same time. You are now exposing your miniature screen!

4 When the timer beeps, turn off the exposure light. Remove the weight and your swatch. You should see that the emulsion in the background has darkened but your image area is lighter because the image positive has resisted the light. Spray, or at least rinse, the test swatch under cold water. In a few minutes, the areas of your image (positive) should start to wash away, and the darkened areas around it (the background) should stay on the screen.

5 Read your exposure swatches. E If the background areas wash away with your image, it is underexposed. Expose the next swatch longer. Try adding a minute. If your image does not wash away but has become hardened with the negative space, it is overexposed. Shorten your exposure time by a minute or so. Keep exposing swatches, adding or subtracting time, fine-tuning until you hit that sweet spot of solid background and crisp, clear image area through which to print.

Cheers to you! Now that you figured out the screen exposure time, you can move on to exposing your screens. For each screen, follow steps 3 through 5 using your calibrated exposure time.

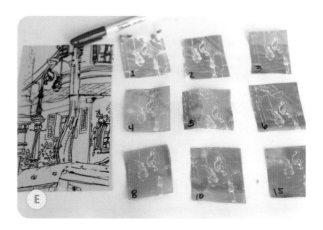

RECLAIMING YOUR SCREEN

After a while, when you are good and tired of an image on the screen, you can reclaim it by washing off the old emulsion. First, check that the screen is still in good shape with no holes or tears and that it is clear of dried ink. If it is really clogged or torn up, you might as well cut the screen out, restretch new mesh, and retape it rather than reclaiming it. If you desire to reclaim it, make sure you buy screen reclaimer that works specifically with your emulsion; I have found that one type does not work well for all emulsions. For convenience, I put the reclaimer in a spray bottle to spray the screen, but you can also pour it or brush it on. Be sure to read the label for safety precautions; some recommend using a respirator, and many do not recommend letting the reclaimer dry on the screen.

YOU WILL NEED:

Work surface

Apron and rubber gloves

Emulsion-coated screen

Screen reclaimer

Spray bottle or paintbrush

Scrub brush

Degreaser: Bon Ami or Comet

INSTRUCTIONS:

1 Wearing your apron and gloves, lay the screen flat out on a table, print side up. Spray or brush the screen with reclaimer and give it a few minutes to start dissolving the emulsion.

2 Scrub the screen with the scrub brush. Rinse the screen in cold water and let dry. Sometimes it takes more than one reclaiming session to remove all of the old emulsion. I get off what I can, rinse and let it dry, then spray and scrub again. You can also spray reclaimer from the squeegee side as needed.

3 When you are ready to reuse the screen, check any spots that may need to be retaped, and then scrub it with Bon Ami or Comet to degrease it. Your screen is ready for its next image!

CHAPTER 5

PLACEMENT, PATTERNS, REPEATS, AND REGISTRATION

Whether you want to be precise or just have fun with it, you likely have some idea of how you want to place your prints. In this chapter, I'll show you how. We'll print some implied patterns, playing with pattern and maneuvering the screen to print all over and wherever you like. We'll also get into some repeat engineering in a few common layouts. Soon you will be able to design and print a screen in measured repeat for a precise, professional look. In fact, by the end of this chapter, you will be able to print just about anything in any configuration that you can dream up!

PLACEMENT PRINTING

Placement printing is the technique of printing a single or a few images on a finished item for their compositional impact, whether the placement is traditional or unconventional. With placement printing, it's pretty easy to eyeball where you would like to print. You have a lot of options: go for symmetry, throw the design off center, size it up and crop it off the side, have fun with it. Here are the main strategies I use.

Front and Center A

You can easily center an image on the front of a T-shirt as shown. I use the components of the tee to place the design, centering the screen between the bottom seam of the sleeves so it is right smack in the middle of the chest.

Asymmetry B

Honestly, I have a lot more fun printing things asymmetrically, off kilter, and making up diagonal lines than arranging things symmetrically. Not only is it more dynamic, it's more forgiving. Be careful not to print just a little off center, just a little crooked, because it will look like you messed up trying print it straight. It should be off enough to look intentional, like you meant to do it, like you designed it that way.

When I print a shirt, I like to carry over the pattern onto the shoulder and down the sleeve, or at the waist, wrapping the design around the side and onto the back. I just made a T-shirt for my mom depicting her old, fat-tired bicycle printed in three or four repeats flying downhill from the right shoulder to the left hip, while a flock of birds flew in the opposite direction, up and over and down her right sleeve. In my Jennythreads line, I adore counterbalancing print with hemlines and making motifs cascade down a dress or flutter up a sleeve.

Size Up C

Is the image bigger than the item you want to print? Excellent! Crop it off the shoulder, wrap it around the side, or rotate it to create more dynamic composition. I love the graphic look of large silhouettes off to the side—on a shoulder of a blouse, on the hip of a skirt. Baby clothes are especially fun to print because even a small image can outsize and take over a boring little outfit, as you can see in the Tough Guy Baby Jumpers on page 132.

Add a Sub-Pattern D

While a large printed motif can command visual attention, a little pattern in the background can add complexity and depth. Work on top of an existing patterned fabric like striped jersey or gingham checks, or print an accompanying motif of your own in a muted color that doesn't compete with the main attraction.

Juxtaposition E

You'll be surprised at what weird and wonderful combinations you can make up. One of my favorite overlapping prints happened when my students and I shared all the screens we had made to print on tank tops. I printed a giraffe drawn by my studio assistant and then printed my student's moose head on its back and suddenly I had a bizarre, two-headed creature that still cracks me up.

IMPLIED REPEAT PATTERNS

Nobody said every pattern you create has to be precise. If you love to print imagery of any shape, whether it is a design that repeats exactly or not, you can print implied patterns. An implied pattern occurs when you print a design repeatedly in a way that tricks the eye into reading it as a pattern. It's a great way to experiment with building up a subtle and richly layered surface, whether with transparent and opaque textile inks, dyes, or even color removers. You'll be surprised at the complexity and nuance you can achieve through layering and varying your overlapping prints. Simply rotating the screen as you print can create dynamic patterns.

Print Implied Repeats

Pin your item and get ready to print.

Start printing (see page 33) and keep on going until you fill the fabric surface. You can vary your placement and patterns greatly. Keep the screen facing one direction, tumble it around, print on the diagonal, place your prints close together, or space them far apart.

Let the first layer dry, and then keep going! Feel free to print multiple screens, colors, and layers to get a feel for this style of printing. Play with pattern like music, with repetition and variation.

TIP *If your screen overlaps the printed areas, it will track the ink around onto the fabric as you print. If it is only on an occasional small bit of a corner, you can place a piece of scrap paper over the print to keep the screen from picking up the ink. Lift the paper and set it aside right after printing. If you are going for a closer print and the screen overlaps it a lot, it could become a real mess, so you may have to print in multiple sessions for each layer. Print repeats with large areas of space between them, dry them completely, and then fill in with fresh prints.*

INTERLOCKING REPEAT MODULES

Since you are working within a rectangular screen, your print window is also rectangular; this dictates the size and shape of your image. But you can work within the screen's print window to print any shape you can dream up. A module is a unit that is repeated to create a pattern, potentially to dazzling and even dizzying effect. Depicted in the patterns shown are just a few repeat modules out of any infinite number of variations. There are geometric shapes: the hexagon or honeycomb, the equilateral triangle, and, of course the square and the rectangle. Two of my favorite organic modules, the ogee and the scale, are geometrically derived and interlock effectively in tessellated structures. The ogee, or onion, is a diamond but with curves that form points at the ends. The scale is also based on a diamond, with concave curved lines capped by a convex line, reminiscent of fish scales, feathers on birds, or repeating fans.

Design an Interlocking Repeat

Once you have drawn one module and want to see how it will look against more repeats on paper, simply make a few photocopies of it, cut them out, and arrange them together into different configurations. You can even group modules together into a larger repeating unit to fit in the print window. Similarly, if you are designing a repeat module on the computer, copy and paste the module into a larger field, copy and paste it again and again, and move the modules into adjacent positions to get an idea of how multiples interact. In either technique, use the information you gain from placing them next to each other to improve and modify your design. Whether you design clean and modern abstract compositions, representational windows of the world, or fun and frilly decorations, consider how the components within them adjoin and change. Once you make the design into a stencil on your screen, you also have the freedom to experiment with placement on the field of fabric, another world of possibilities.

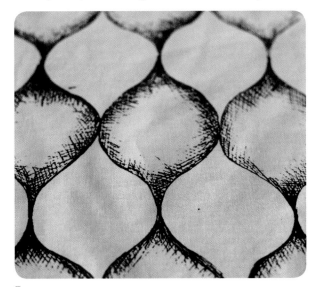

▌ An ogee repeat.

▌ A scale repeat.

MEASURED REPEAT PATTERNS

Looking around my own house and wardrobe, it's easy to see that my favorite print patterns are in two colors: the motif and the background. I think this is simply because two-color print palettes are easier to mix with others in larger groupings, whether throwing a few pillows on a sofa or layering an embellished cardigan over a silk blouse. When you are just getting started with printing in measured repeat, I recommend printing exactly that: one color on a background fabric. And then, if you want more of a challenge, try your hand at registering multiple screens together (see this technique on page 82). Working with repeats requires some careful measuring, marking, and paying attention to those marks to position the screen correctly. But there's no real tricky math involved. As with any skill, the more you do it, the easier it becomes.

Tools and Materials

CARPENTER'S SPEED SQUARE: Also known as a rafter angle square, a speed square is actually a right triangle made of metal. Pick one up at the hardware store. It has different gradated rulers along its sides that aid carpenters in calculating trigonometric roof angles, which is beyond the scope of repeat printing. Handy for our application, however, is that one side of the triangle is a 7-inch (17.8 cm) ruler, and along the adjacent side is a ledge that hooks right around the side of a screen frame. It is very helpful when lining up stencils on screens for precise registration.

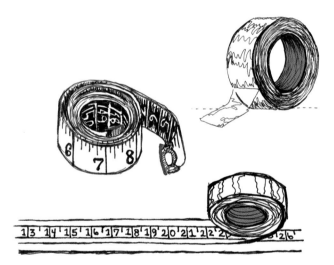

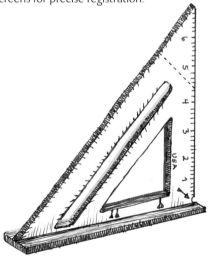

DRESSMAKER'S MEASURING TAPE AND CLEAR PACK-ING TAPE: Your measuring tape should be the length of your printing surface. Establish a vertical ruler along the length of the print table. Center the dressmaker's measuring tape so that it is encased within the packing tape and affix them together to the print table as shown.

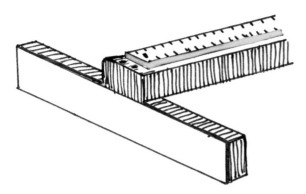

T-SQUARE WITH METAL RULER: This is a beefier model than the ones architects used to use for drafting (before there were CAD computer programs). The purpose of the T-square is to act as a straight and sturdy guide against which you will place the screen and mark the horizontal increments for printing. I built mine out of two 2 x 4 boards set at a right angle and screwed the metal ruler along the top.

GREASE PENCILS: Also known as china markers, soft wax-based grease pencils are ideal for marking on slick and glossy surfaces. For our purposes, you will see they are handy for marking screen positions on our improvised grid of packing tape and a T-square ruler. Plus they are easy to erase by wiping the marked surface vigorously with an old towel. Since we will employ some color coding for screen placements, I recommend picking up two different colored grease pencils.

PREWASHED FABRIC CUT TO SIZE: The size of fabric yardage you can print in measured repeat is limited by the size of your print table. If you are printing measured repeats or registering multiple screens on yardage longer than your print table, you should either cut your fabric into pieces that fit on the table or work in table-length sections of your yardage, leaving a little bit of space between the printed fields. It would be a logistical nightmare to stretch, pin, measure, and print separate sections of fabric and then try to align them next to each other seamlessly; it's not worth the attempt. That's why fabric screenprinters have really long print tables.

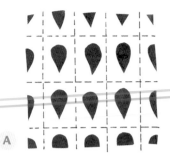
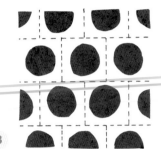
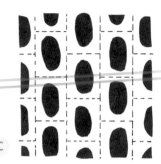

Modular Repetition

Pattern is inevitable in screenprinting because once you've got a screen with a stencil on it and you pull your first print, you'll want to keep going. I find pattern in nature absolutely fascinating: in the brindle stripes of my dog Rosco, the variegated feathers of neighbors' chickens, the branches of winter trees, the seeded surface of a strawberry. Just as inspiring, I have an antique quilt from the 1930s—a double wedding ring pattern on a field of bubblegum pink cotton. I get mesmerized by the dozens of vintage print fabrics pieced together that compose it: rough and tumble puppies, crisp art deco geometrics, sweet little ditzy florals. I look at it from afar, admiring the way the paths of squares have the same cool tones and read like one surface, which makes the bubblegum pink pop so effectively. All these details, whether from nature or the hands of an unknown quilter, inspire me to create more intricate and clever patterns.

SQUARE REPEAT: This repeat is a simple grid layout. More sophisticated than the grid repeat are the brick and half-drop repeats. **A**

BRICK REPEAT: This layout is just as it sounds, like a brick wall. Brick repeat is a horizontal pattern, which conveys a calm sturdiness and structure. Depending on the motifs you print, it can reference the lay of the land, clouds over a mountain ridge, sand dunes, ocean waves, or the figure in repose. **B**

HALF-DROP REPEAT: In this repeat, each vertical column is staggered, dropped half a step lower than the one beside it. Vertical layouts can convey more energy: the direction plants and trees grow; the figure upright, at attention, on guard. **C**

DESIGN A REPEAT MODULE (FOR SQUARE, BRICK, AND HALF-DROP LAYOUTS)

This is a quick and easy way to design the elements within a geometric module to align perfectly in repeat. The perimeter is where the module meets up with others, so where you end a line at the edge of one, it will continue onto the adjoining module. If you are going to print each module individually, make the original the size of your print window. Remember, you can make the perimeter of each module a prominent part of the design or camouflage it to make it practically invisible. I'll show you how to design (and print on page 78) in three common layouts: square, brick, and half drop. So consider these layouts when you are deciding patterns to print. Bedding? Brick. Wallpaper? Half drop. Oh, but brick would be more calming. It's all arbitrary, really, and it is completely up to you. We'll start with the basic square repeat and then move on to the brick and half-drop repeats. I'm working with a rectangle, though the same principle of lining up parallel sides that will align in repeat can be applied to other parallelograms.

YOU WILL NEED:

Scissors

Paper

Drawing medium of your choice

INSTRUCTIONS:

Instructions for a Square Repeat

1 Cut the paper to the size and shape of one module and start drawing on two sides. **A**

2 Anything you draw along the left side will connect to the right side of the adjacent module once they are put into square repeat. So whenever you draw a line along the left side, fold the paper around so the right side is next to it and continue the drawing. **B**

3 Likewise, anything you draw on the bottom will connect to the top of the adjacent module. Draw a line or shape

touching the bottom edge of the module. Fold the paper to bring the bottom edge to meet with the top. Continue the drawing over the two edges. **C**

4 Continue drawing to fill out the center space of the module. **D**

A

B

C

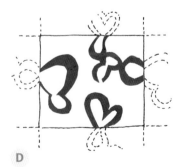

D

Instructions for Brick and Half-Drop Repeats

Each of these are diagonal repeats that align on two sides and are staggered on the other two sides, so the same alignment procedure works for either one. I chose to work with the brick repeat; to work with half-drop, just turn it 90°.

1 Cut the paper to the size and shape of one module.  **A** The module still adjoins evenly on two sides. On the brick repeat, the module lines up with its neighbors on the sides. So whenever you draw a line along the left side, fold the paper around so the right side is next to it and continue the drawing. **B**

> **NOTE** *On the half drop, the module lines up with its neighbors at the top and bottom. Anything you draw on the top will connect to the bottom of the adjacent module. So whenever you draw a line along the top, fold the paper around to bring the bottom edge to meet with the top.*

2 Mark the center of the two sides that will be staggered. On the brick, it's the top and bottom sides. On the half drop, it's the left and right sides. Cut the module in half down the center, parallel to the sides with the marks. This is shown as the dotted line in figure. **C**

3 Stagger the two pieces at their edges how they will repeat, first at one edge as shown. Draw the design from one piece onto the other over the seam. **D**

4 Move the pieces to line up the other two adjoining edges. Draw the design from one piece onto the other. **E**

5 Once you have drawn the design to continue from one corner to the other, tape the module back together where it was originally cut. Now you've got the layout figured out to flow seamlessly from one to the next! **F**

6 Trace or make a photocopy of the draft module onto a fresh sheet of paper, cleaning up any ambiguous areas. At this point, your module is simply a drawing on paper and not necessarily in the stencil form ready for printing.

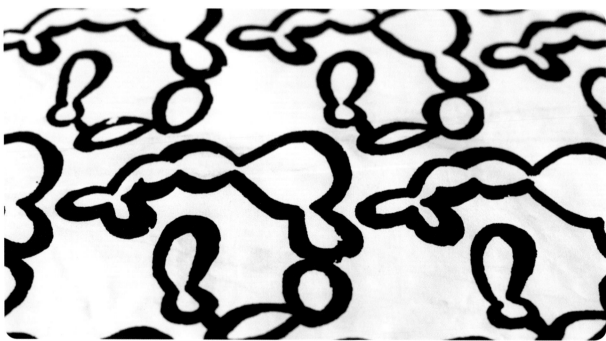

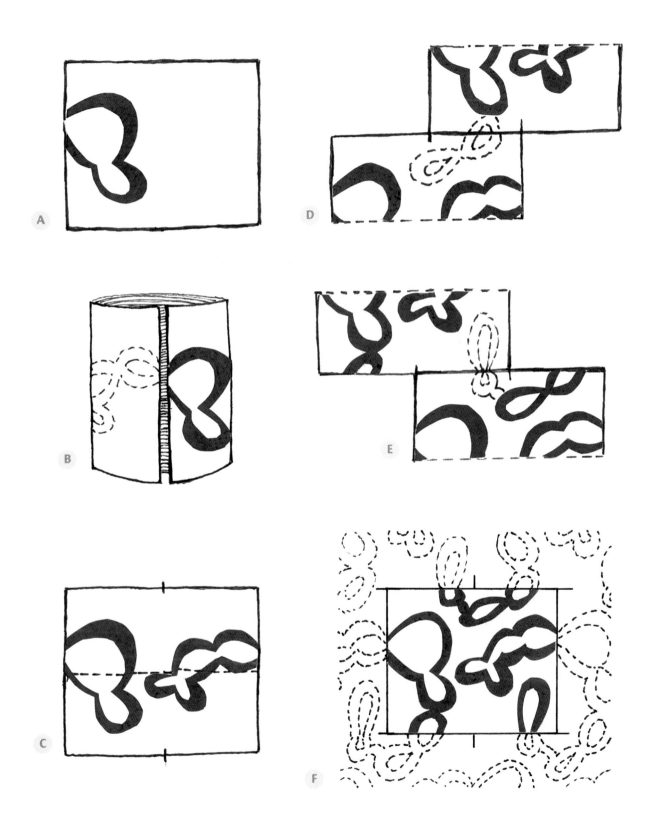

PRINT SQUARE, BRICK, AND HALF-DROP REPEATS

In a way, printing in measured repeat sounds a lot like playing Battleship, only without sinking anyone's destroyer or torpedo sound effects. We'll use the same reference system: a grid with numbers running across one side and letters down the other to plot and locate positions like B1 and G4 for printing. Feel free to make up your own sound effects as you go.

YOU WILL NEED:

Print table or printing board set up on a sturdy table, with dressmaker's measuring tape at least the length of the printing area and clear packing tape

Ruler or measuring tape for measuring your design

Note paper and pencil

Pins

Prewashed fabric to print

Clean, dry, and taped screen with stencil

T-square with metal ruler

Grease pencil to mark printing increments

Apron

Squeegee

Plenty of textile ink

Gloves (optional)

Hair dryer

INSTRUCTIONS:

Square Repeat

1   Measure the height and width of your design, including whether you would like any space between it and the next repeat. The height is your *vertical repeat increment*, and the width is your *horizontal repeat increment*. Jot them down somewhere nearby—you'll need them!

2   Pin your fabric onto your print board and place the screen in the top left corner of the fabric exactly where you would like the first print to go. With a grease pencil, mark an X on the lower right corner of the screen; this will help you keep track of the position and alignment of the screen. Set the T-square against the side of the print table and across the fabric next to the screen. Mark the edge of the X corner on the T-square ruler in grease pencil as well. This is your first horizontal registration mark, so let's be logical and assign it the number 1. Using your horizontal repeat measurement you jotted down, make incremental marks in grease pencil on the T-square ruler all the way to the end, even beyond the width of your fabric. Number them sequentially 2, 3, 4, and so on.

3   Using the same first position of the screen, mark the outside position of the T-square on the vertical ruler (the measuring tape). This is your first vertical registration mark, so we'll assign it row A. Mark vertical increments alphabetically along the entire measuring tape and even beyond the length of your fabric. Once all the marks have been made, put on your apron, grab a squeegee, and be sure you have plenty of ink. For a primer on pulling a print, see page 33.

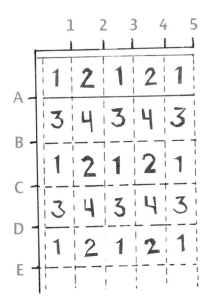

4 First print session (all blocks numbered 1 in the illustration): Place your screen in the A1 position and pull your first print (page 33); lift the screen. Leave the T-square in place. To keep the screen from smearing the fresh print, skip the next mark (2) on the T-square ruler and align the screen with the one after that (3) and print, skip (4) then align and print A5, and so on. Skip the next row (B) entirely and move the T-square so it lines up with the third vertical mark, C. Repeat the 1, 3, 5, etc. screen positions along the T-square to print the C row: C1, C3, C5, and to the end of the row. Continue skipping rows and printing at alternate marks down the entire table according to the illustration: E1, E3, E5, G1, G3, G5, etc.

5 Second print session (all blocks numbered 2 in the illustration): Once the first session's prints are dry, fill in the rows you just printed. Line the T-square and screen back to its position to print row A, and place the screen in the A2 position and print. Leave the T-square in place, and move on to print A4, A6, and so on. Then move to T-square to align and print row C2, C4, C6, on to E2, E4, E6, and so on.

6 Third print session (all blocks numbered 3 in the illustration): When those prints are dry, move the T-square to the second row (B) and print B1. Skip B2 to print B3, skip B4 to print B5, then move to D1, D3, and on to F1, F3, etc., skipping rows and alternating marks.

7 Fourth print session (all blocks numbered 4 in the illustration): Once the third session prints are dry, fill in the remaining blocks in the same manner—start with B2, and continue with B4, D2, D4, and so on—until you've printed all the fabric.

8 Dry the last set of prints, remove the pins, heat-set it, and give it a big hug! It's all yours!

Now that you've got the gist of printing in measured repeat, we'll move on to printing in two variations: the brick and half-drop repeat layouts. Brick and half drop both operate on the same principle since each repeat design is staggered. Here you will be shifting one set of screen positions, either the horizontal measurement on the T-square for the brick, or the vertical measurements on the measuring tape for the half drop.

NOTE *Remember to rinse your screen and dry your prints with the hair dryer after each printing session. Also, keep the T-square itself flush against the side of the print table so your print design doesn't shift with it.*

Brick Repeat

On a brick repeat, the horizontal row stays the same, but the vertical alignment is staggered like, of course, a brick wall. In my illustration, the screen is placed in a horizontal orientation to mimic a brick wall, but the layout procedure is exactly the same for a vertically oriented screen, such as my ribbon motif for the Prize Winner Pet Bed on page 135. You'll see that the first two print sessions align with all the even-numbered marks and then the second two sessions align with all the odd-numbered marks. You'll see that as you print, the even- and odd-numbered rows are staggered— that's the brick!

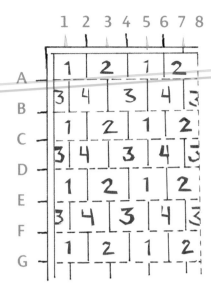

1 Pin down your fabric on the print table and then place the screen exactly how you would like it to print in the top left position. Measure and mark both the horizontal repeats and vertical repeats just like you did for the square repeat layout (page 78).

2 Using the same horizontal repeat measurement, make marks (yellow in the illustration) halfway between and beyond the previous marks. Then number all the marks, starting with "1" in the left corner. Grab your apron, squeegee, and plenty of ink to start printing.

3 First printing session: Start with your screen in the A2 position (the A1 is a half-step to the left of the top corner and is not printed). Pull your first print and lift the screen. Leave the T-square in place and skip A4 to align and print A6 and so on, if necessary, to skip A8 to align and print A10. See, you are printing every other even-numbered mark in the A row. Skip the second row, B, and move the T-square to C row. Print C2, skip C4 to align and print C6, and on to C10 if necessary, then on to E2, E6, etc. Continue printing every other row and every other repeat for all the blocks numbered 1.

4 Once these are dry, fill in the even-numbered positions in each row in your second print session. Bring the T-square back up to row A and align the screen to A4 and print, then skip to A8. Move the T-square to row C, printing C4 and C8, continuing to fill in rows E, G, and so on for all the blocks numbered 2. Dry all prints completely.

5 Next, in your third print session, align the T-square with row B1, which crops halfway off the left side of the fabric. Pull the print, keep the T-square in place, skip B3 to align and print B5, and skip B7 to align and print B9, which crops halfway off the other side of the fabric

(every other odd-numbered mark). Move the T-square down to align and print every other row and every other odd-numbered repeat: D1, D5, D9, F1, F5, F9, and so on.

6 Once these are dry, move the T-square back up to row B to fill it in, aligning and printing B3 and B7. Continue printing alternating rows with the remaining odd-numbered marks, printing D3, D7, F3, F7, (printing all the blocks numbered 4) and so on to complete the yardage.

7 Once all of your prints are dry, remove the pins, pick up the fabric, and heat-set it. Now you've printed your very own dreamy yardage in a brick repeat!

Half-Drop Repeat

On a half-drop repeat, the prints fall into vertical columns whose horizontal alignment with each other is staggered. So like the brick repeat, you will be alternating even and odd prints, but on the opposite axis.

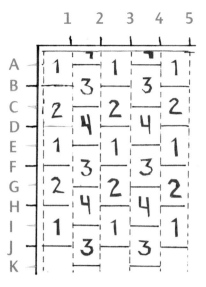

1   Pin down your fabric on the print table and then place the screen exactly how you would like it to print in the top left position. Measure and mark both the horizontal repeats and vertical repeats just like you did the square-repeat layout (page 78).

2   Using the same vertical repeat measurement, make marks halfway between the previous marks (shown in the illustration in yellow) on the tape measure, Additionally, make a mark halfway above the first black mark to be sure the repeat continues in both directions. Mark the horizontal marks numerically from left to right starting with 1. Mark the vertical positions alphabetically starting with A. Now that you've made the marks, grab your squeegee and ink to print.

3   Print session 1: Place the T-square to print the B row, and the screen in B1. Pull your first print and lift the screen. Leave the T-square in place and alternate prints in the row: Skip B2 to print B3, skip B4 to print B5, and so on. Move the T-square to skip row D to align and print row F, printing F1, F3, and F5. Skip row H to align and print row J, with J1, J3, J5, and so on. Continue printing every other repeat in the columns to print all blocks numbered 1.

4   Once they are dry, fill in the columns with print session 2. Place the T-square to print row D, starting with D1. Leave the T-square in place to align and print D3 and D5. Move the T-square to align and print row H, printing H1, H3, and H5, completing the odd-numbered columns. Dry them completely.

5   For the third session, you will start printing the remaining (even-numbered) columns, one-half step down—that's the half-drop! Place the T-square on row C, and the screen on C2, pull the print and leave the T-square in place. Skip to the next even-numbered mark, C4 (and on to C6, C8, etc., if necessary). Move the T-square to skip to row E and print G2, G4, etc., and down to K2, K4, and so on. Dry your prints completely.

6   For the fourth session, you are filling in the last prints to complete the half-dropped columns. Bring the T-square up to row A and print A2. Leave the T-square in place to print A4, and so on, which will crop off the top of the fabric. Move the T-square to row E to print E2, E4, and so on, then on to I2 and I4, and so on. You've got it!

Take a few minutes to admire the bright, chipper, and oh-so-clever half-drop yardage you have printed!

REGISTER MULTIPLE SCREENS TO PRINT TOGETHER IN REPEAT

Once you have been printing for a while and want to get into registration that is more precise than just eyeballing multiple screens to layer together, try printing with two registered screens in repeat. It is important to measure precisely and to match the position of the imagery on each screen so they line up when printed. Be sure that your screen is straight and square; if it is worn out and wonky, your design will be skewed. If you are using commercially made screens that are in good condition, you should be fine. It is easiest to work with two identically sized screens with matching print windows. But if that is not the case, you can still make it work, because you can work off one corner to align them.

YOU WILL NEED:

Print table or printing board set up on a sturdy table, with dressmaker's measuring tape at least the length of the printing area and clear packing tape

Two clean, dry, and taped screens in matching, or at least, similar size

Grease pencil for marking on the screen frame

Fine-point permanent marker for marking on the screen within the print window

Pencil for figuring measurements

Ruler or carpenter's speed square

Stencil or image positive to fit inside print windows on all screens

Masking tape

Photo emulsion (page 53; optional)

Pins

Prewashed fabric to print

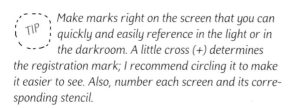

TIP *Make marks right on the screen that you can quickly and easily reference in the light or in the darkroom. A little cross (+) determines the registration mark; I recommend circling it to make it easier to see. Also, number each screen and its corresponding stencil.*

INSTRUCTIONS:

1 Lay out all screens in the same orientation. Choose a corner from which to anchor your design and base all your measurements for registering and printing your artwork. On each screen, draw an X in grease pencil on that same corner on both the print and squeegee sides of the screen. **A**

2 Use the ruler or speed square to figure where to place a registration mark in three corners of the print window at least ¼ inch (.6 cm) within the print window. Measure from the bottom and side (the corner with the directional marks) and decide on a distance; as an example, I used 3 inches (7.6 cm). Measure from the outside of the screen frame to the edge of the stencil. Measure it in two spots on the side so it is exactly 3 inches (7.6 cm) from the frame edge and exactly parallel to the frame edge on both of those sides. Each of these should be outside of the artwork, and within the smallest dimension of all of your print windows. This takes a bit of measuring and double-checking to make sure it is correct. These will be consistent on all screens, measuring out from the X corner. To make the three marks, draw small crosses along the ruler with a fine-point marker directly on the screen mesh at the designated 3-inch (7.6 cm) square corners. **B**

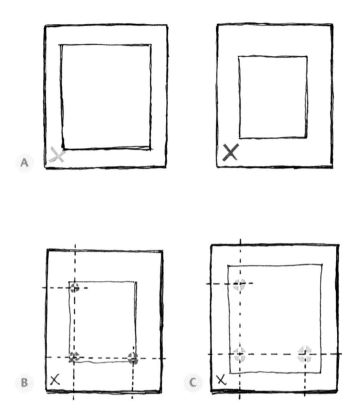

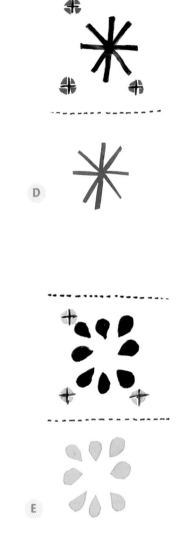

3 Using the exact same measurements from the same X corner as you did the first screen, make the same three registration marks on the next screen. Repeat for any additional screens in the sequence. **C**

4 With your first screen print side up, place your first stencil on its screen in the orientation and position you would like it to print. Use a little masking tape to tape it in place so it doesn't shift around. Trace the registration marks from the screen onto the stencil. Then place your next stencil on top of the first one and align it exactly how you would like them to print together. Trace the registration marks from the first stencil onto the second one. Repeat for any additional stencils in the sequence. **D** **E**

NOTE *Be sure to scale your artwork to fit inside the smallest print-window dimensions. You will need to measure all screens involved and figure the smallest height and width dimensions of the print windows. The size of the image plus the area for registration marks must be smaller than the smallest print window. If the width of the print window is smaller on one screen while the height is smaller on the other screen, use a stencil or image positive that will fit inside the smallest dimensions. In my illustrations, I work with two screens of different sizes with different print windows to show how to handle just such a situation.*

5   Adhere each stencil to its screen for printing, being very careful to line them up at all three registration marks. If you are using photo emulsion, you will line them up in the darkroom and align all the registration marks on the image positives with those on the screen in the exact same manner, then shoot and spray them out (see page 62). F G Once all the stencils are on the screens, it's time to print!

6   Set up and print all of the repeats of the first layer in whatever measured repeat your heart desires. Square repeat is on page 78, brick repeat is on page 80, and half-drop repeat is on page 81. Leave the fabric pinned down to the print table. Once it is dry, you can start lining up the second screen to print. However, don't assume that your screens will line up perfectly at the same registration marks. I know you measured very carefully, but trust me—it's worth double-checking!

7   Place the new screen in the first print position according to your working layout and look closely at whether the screen stencil lines up with the previously printed image. Check that the X corner of the screen lines up with the first mark and the T-square is in line with the first vertical marks. If both line up perfectly, you're in luck. You can skip step 8 and start printing on step 9. But if either one doesn't line up, even if it's off by a fraction of an inch, you need to measure and make new registration marks for this screen. Take the few minutes and do it; it's worth the time and effort to get it right.

8   Wipe away the grease pencil marks you made on the ruler and measuring tape for the previous print. Use those marks to align your second screen in place to overlap perfectly with the first prints.

9   Print the second screen right on top of the first prints. Work in the same order and number of printing sessions as you did the first screen.

F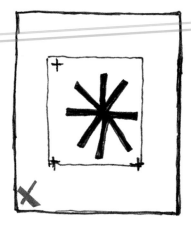

G

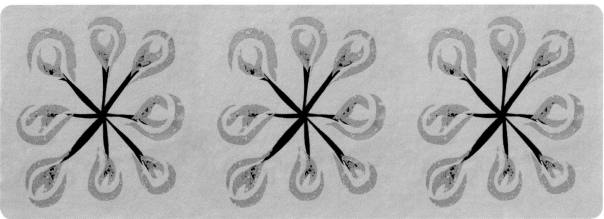

Here you can see the two screens and the fabric printed in repeat.

CHAPTER 6

BEYOND INK

Why would you want to bother with dyes when there are so many color possibilities with textile inks? Well, textile ink acts much like paint on the surface of the fabric. Dyes, on the other hand, work at the molecular level—they react chemically, and the color becomes an integral part of the fabric itself. So you can achieve greater richness and a depth of color not possible with inks while maintaining the "hand" of the fabric—its natural feel, weight, and drape. The processes described in this chapter require some safety precautions and enough attention to follow a recipe just as if you were cooking. You will have a few more steps and safeguards than you do working with textile inks, but it will be worth it.

SAFELY HANDLING DYES AND RELATED CHEMICALS

So far we have been working with pretty benign products—textile inks, screen filler, even photo emulsion—all in liquid form and at room temperature, and we haven't had to pull out the respiratory safety gear I advised you to round up way back in chapter 2. Well, now is the time to whip out the respirator, the dust mask, the apron, and the long gloves. I'd like to mention a few other precautions when working with dyes and discharge agents as well.

USE DEDICATED EQUIPMENT: The main thing is to keep dyeing equipment separate from your food-ingesting space. Plenty of times I've improvised chopsticks from two pencils rather than eating with a dye-mixing spoon! If you pull anything from your household kitchen, don't put it back! It's now a dye studio utensil, never to be used for food again.

LABEL IT: The dye studio is not the place for mystery concoctions, so label everything you use and mix. Keep your dyeing supplies and utensils organized and in their own storage area or cabinet out of the reach of children and pets. I can't imagine a kid wanting to eat some powdered dye; maybe he'd just dump it out and smear it on the walls. Either way, it's not pretty.

ENSURE PROPER VENTILATION: Work in the best ventilation possible—work outside on nice days, work near a window with a fan facing outward to blow dust and fumes outside. If you need to steam fabric printed with dye or thiox, do it on a hot plate set on the porch; don't use your kitchen stove top. In my studio, I set up the dye heating and steaming area in the bathroom. Then I can keep the door closed and let the exhaust fan carry the fumes directly outside.

DISPOSE OF MIXED DYES AND DYE BATHS PROPERLY: Neutralize dye and discharge solutions with a little something from the opposite side of the pH scale (see page 91). If you are dumping an acid bath, first stir in a teaspoon of soda ash. Likewise, if you are about to dump an alkaline bath, pour in a little vinegar. The acid and base will react together and cancel each other out; it will foam up for a few seconds, so keep your face away from it. One exception to this rule is common household chlorine bleach. Adding acid to bleach can create hazardous gases, so it should be neutralized with hydrogen peroxide or antichlor (more about that on page 93). Pour your old solutions down the drain into the sewer line, where it can be processed by municipal waste management systems rather than dumping it in the street or your yard, where it will flow who knows where.

TOOLS AND MATERIALS

In this chapter, we'll get into more involved recipes beyond mixing inks; accordingly, we'll need some additional implements and supplies. It is important to mix ingredients carefully and accurately. Like I mentioned earlier, once items are used for dyes and other chemicals, do not reintroduce them into your home kitchen.

Basics

WIRE WHISK: Perfect for breaking up hard-to-dissolve dyes, clumpy thickeners, and quickly achieving smooth consistencies, the whisk is my favorite mixing tool. Not only is it more efficient than a spoon and a whole lot easier to clean than a blender, it's also a really fun little object to draw.

OTHER KITCHEN IMPLEMENTS FOR DYEING: In addition to the handy dandy wire whisk, you'll need a few basic tools for mixing and measuring, like measuring cups and spoons, small containers, squeeze bottles, funnels, and resealable pitchers with lids. For immersion dyeing at the end of the chapter, you'll need a few small buckets and bowls. Refer to the recipes ahead for specifics.

Fiber Reactive Dyes

There are many different families of dyes relevant to the fibers with which they bond. In this chapter, we will be working with fiber reactive Procion MX dyes. This popular dye family is simple and user friendly, colorfast (does not fade with washing), and works in room-temperature water

so it does not have to be heated to a boil. MX dyes are terrific for immersion dyeing and direct painting, and they can be thickened for screenprinting on fabric. While the vast array of color choices can be overwhelming, I recommend getting a fiber reactive dye sampler or starter kit. These kits include a few primary dye colors along with the auxiliary chemicals that make them work. MX dyes are man-made, but they are specifically formulated to react with natural fibers derived from plants or animals. Like a square peg will not fit in a round hole, a dye developed for natural fibers will not magically dye polyester simply because you heated it to the boiling point or soaked it for a week. It is not a matter of time or strength, but of chemistry.

MX dyes are very uncomplicated with a forgiving margin of error! I am not much of a measurer, and I can get pretty consistent results, but I've had lots and lots of experience (I've even dyed garments to match paint swatches by sight). So if you are new to the process, measure! Also, keep track of what you are doing and write down formulas and steps as you go for reference later. With more experience, it will become more intuitive.

Color Removers, aka Discharge Agents

It's almost magical to print with a color remover, creating a light pattern on a colored ground; this is how I print most of the yardage for my Jennythreads clothing line. Discharge agents remove the colors of dyed fabrics in a chemical process with the dye molecules themselves. Keep in mind that textile inks, which are printed on the surface of the fabric, are not vulnerable to the discharge process. With all discharge processes, fumes can be at best stinky and at worst toxic, so you will need to work in a well-ventilated area and wear a respirator with filter cartridges specifically for vapors.

The fascinating part is that discharging hardly ever returns the fabric color to white or its original color. Each fabric and dye lightens to a different color, some respond better than others, and some don't respond to discharge at all. Red could turn to pink or yellow, blue turns to gray or orange, purple turns to aqua, and there are always surprises. Some colors are more stubborn than others! Commercially dyed black is notorious for being very difficult to discharge; turquoise is also tough.

DISCHARGE PASTE: If you want a quick and easy way to try printing with a color remover that is safe for both plant and animal fibers, then get some discharge paste. This is a sulfur-based chemical with a long name—sodium formaldehyde sulfoxylate—which has already been thickened and activated, and is ready to print right out of the bottle. After printing, you must allow it to dry, steam it in a pot or with a steam iron to activate the color removal activity, and then wash the paste out of the fabric. It is odorless while printing but then smells nasty during steaming. I find that its premixed formula can also be a disadvantage; if you print with it and get lackluster results, you can't make it stronger. For this reason, I prefer mixing and printing with thiourea dioxide.

THIOUREA DIOXIDE: Nicknamed thiox, thiourea dioxide is safe to use on plant and animal fibers. It smells awful, like someone is getting a perm with a basket of rotten eggs at their feet. The jury is still out about the long-term effects of inhaling thiox fumes, so wear a respirator with filter cartridges specific to vapors and work in a well-ventilated area. Thiox is available from dye suppliers, arrives in a yellowish white powder form, and must be dissolved in hot water, activated with soda ash, and thickened with sodium alginate to print. Like discharge paste, thiox must be allowed to dry and then steamed to make the color change. The stronger it is mixed and the hotter it gets, the more dramatic the color removal. I am partial to thiox because my recipe is very simple, and it is highly effective for discharging fiber reactive dyes on a production scale.

CHLORINE BLEACH: Household chlorine bleach is available wherever cleaning products are sold, from the grocery store to the hardware store. I think of chlorine bleach as a super villain, relentlessly firing a big death ray, aggressively working to destroy. It is highly reactive, oxidizing everything in its path, and it will continue to break down the fibers of the fabric once it has broken down the dye color. But never fear, it can be neutralized and then washed as usual. It is effective on a wider array of dye families than discharge paste or thiox, but it is also destructive to many more fibers. Bleach is ideal to use on 100 percent plant fibers such as cotton, linen, or hemp, but it breaks down animal fibers like silk and wool and even many synthetics.

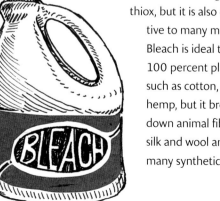

Activators

An activator is the agent that locks the dye color together with the fiber. You will need an activator for all the dyeing I'll show you in this chapter—there's no escaping it. Activators affect the pH of the dye solution and are fiber specific: acids are ideal for protein (animal) fibers such as silk and wool, and alkalis are best for cellulose (plant) fibers such as cotton and linen.

VINEGAR AND CITRIC ACID CRYSTALS: Acid ingredients are the activators for dyeing protein fibers such as silk and wool. For printing dyes, you will need a concentrated, solid acid that won't dilute your dye printing solution, so I recommend using citric acid crystals, available from the dye suppliers. For immersion dyeing on silk, I use good old white vinegar as my acid activator, buying five or six gallons at a time. The checkout lady at the grocery store started calling me the Pickle Queen until I finally told her what I do for a living, but the nickname stuck.

SODA ASH: Alkaline ingredients are used to activate dyes on plant fibers such as cotton as well as the color remover thiox. I use soda ash (sodium carbonate), also known as washing soda, a stronger cousin of baking soda. Soda ash is available from the dye suppliers or even in the pool-care section of the hardware store. You can get away with soda ash for dyeing silk in a pinch, but you'll get significantly better color yields by using acid on silk instead.

Auxiliaries

Auxiliaries are related ingredients that help with the dyeing, discharge, and printing processes. It's easy to get overwhelmed with all the auxiliaries when you start working with dyes. If you go on the website for any major dye supplier, you'll see a myriad of auxiliary chemicals for all sorts of purposes: retaining color, reviving texture, making it softer, making it stiffer, potions and lotions to coax and

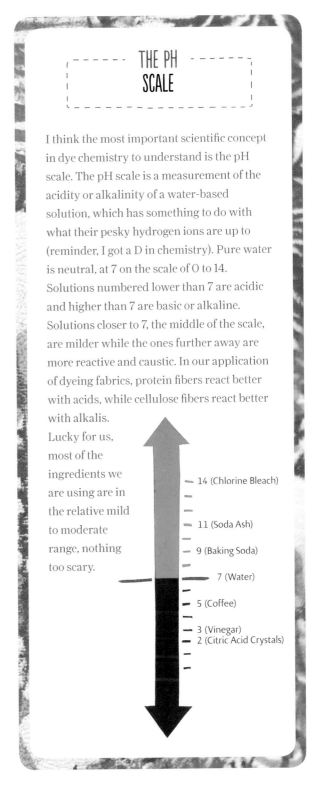

THE PH SCALE

I think the most important scientific concept in dye chemistry to understand is the pH scale. The pH scale is a measurement of the acidity or alkalinity of a water-based solution, which has something to do with what their pesky hydrogen ions are up to (reminder, I got a D in chemistry). Pure water is neutral, at 7 on the scale of 0 to 14. Solutions numbered lower than 7 are acidic and higher than 7 are basic or alkaline. Solutions closer to 7, the middle of the scale, are milder while the ones further away are more reactive and caustic. In our application of dyeing fabrics, protein fibers react better with acids, while cellulose fibers react better with alkalis. Lucky for us, most of the ingredients we are using are in the relative mild to moderate range, nothing too scary.

14 (Chlorine Bleach)

11 (Soda Ash)

9 (Baking Soda)

7 (Water)

5 (Coffee)

3 (Vinegar)
2 (Citric Acid Crystals)

cajole the fabric before and after the chemical reactions and to make your dyes take the color. Listen, you just need a few components to do it beautifully and efficiently. I have decent tap water and a good success rate, so I just stick with these basic ingredients; it works fine for me and it should for you, too. Then if you want to try some fancy new product, go on and give it a whirl!

SYNTHRAPOL: This is a detergent specifically for use with fabric at two important stages of the dyeing process: the prewash and after dyeing. Add a little Synthrapol to the prewash to scour the fabric, and remove any dirt, oil, finishes, sizing, and other impurities that can interfere with the dye process. Then, after you have dyed or printed the fabric, you'll need to wash it once more with Synthrapol in hot water to get rid of excess dyes, activators, thickeners, and to restore it to its natural yet newly colored state. Synthrapol is a pH neutral surfactant, so it doesn't continue to activate the dyes, instead keeping them in solution so they don't attach themselves to unintended areas during the wash. If your fabric is prepared for dyeing, or PFD, you can probably skip the scouring step. But if you need to preshrink the fabric before dyeing it anyway, combine your steps by adding a little Synthrapol to the wash to scour the fabric as well.

UREA: When dye molecules are in a dye bath, we can imagine them floating and migrating around in the water to bond with the fibers, having lots of time and space to get the whole operation good and done. But when you thicken and print with dyes in the open air, there is a lot less moisture for the dyes to move around in, and the dyeing environment dries out much more quickly, sometimes before the color bonding process can happen. Urea serves as a humectant, or a water attractor, so adding it to the water in which the dyes are mixed gives them and the fiber more time to properly react and bond, yielding more intense colors.

You'll notice in my recipes that I add urea to different solutions, and I have my reasons. Urea water is handy for dissolving the urea with powder dyes right before thickening them, as well as for painting with the dyes directly on the fabric. If you are using dye stock solutions, which are simply dye dissolved in water, you can add the urea to your sodium alginate thickener paste when you are ready to print. Really, you just want to make sure it gets into the mix with the dye somewhere before printing. Alternatively, if you are using sodium alginate thickener paste that already has urea premixed into it, you can skip this step altogether.

METAPHOS: This is the product name for sodium hexam-etaphospate. It is an optional water softener that is added to urea water to keep the minerals in very hard water from interfering with the dye process.

SODIUM ALGINATE: Obviously dye solutions, like color concentrates, are not thick enough to screenprint, so they must be thickened. Sodium alginate is perfect for the job. Made from ground seaweed, it is also listed as an ingredient in many food items, but I don't advise you to eat your thickener paste! It is available in powder form, which you must then mix with water to create a gelatin-like substance to add to the dye for printing. Sodium alginate is available in two viscosities: formula F (low viscosity, thinner, and more pourable) for silk, which also works with other animal fibers, and formula SH (high viscosity, thicker, and less pourable) for cotton, also appropriate for other plant fibers. Once it is mixed with water, sodium alginate lasts about a week or two at room temperature and up to a month or so in the fridge, then it breaks down and starts to stink. Once this happens, you can't use it, so just pour it down the sink and mix up a new batch.

NOTE *For printing specifically with dyes, I recommend getting sodium alginate that is premixed with other auxiliary chemicals like urea, metaphos, and Ludigol versus plain old sodium alginate. As you'll see, plain old sodium alginate is my thickener of choice for printing with the discharge agent thiox, which we will get to on page 101.*

MONAGUM: Chlorine bleach is such a strong oxidizer that it breaks down sodium alginate too quickly for screenprinting. Instead, you'll need to thicken it with monagum, the product name for carboxymethyl starch, another powdered auxiliary chemical available from dye suppliers. You'll mix the monagum with water, and, like sodium alginate, it thickens into a paste to mix with bleach right before printing.

HYDROGEN PEROXIDE 3% AND ANTICHLOR: While discharge paste and thiox are heat activated after printing, chlorine bleach starts working on its own as soon as it comes in contact with the fabric and must be neutralized to stop. A common neutralizing chemical from the dye suppliers is bisulfite, known by the product name antichlor. Or hydrogen peroxide 3% from the pharmacy works as well; I use about one 16-ounce bottle per yard of printed fabric.

NOTE *Acids such as vinegar should never, ever be used to neutralize chlorine bleach! The two react to create dangerous chlorine gas. Stick with antichlor or hydrogen peroxide 3% to neutralize bleach.*

Steamers

Steaming fabric sets the dye color and activates color removal. There are four options for steaming fabric: iron it with steam, or rig up a steamer of your own in a cook pot on the stove top, in a box steamer, or a bullet steamer. Either way, you'll need to protect your fabric in steaming cloths.

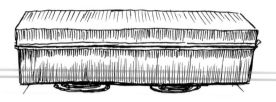

STEAMING CLOTH OR NEWSPRINT: Steaming sets the dye colors, but drops of water that form inside the steamer can cause your freshly printed colors to bleed and run. You need to sandwich the fabric between cotton steaming cloths or paper to separate the layers so they don't bleed onto each other. For steaming and pressing cloths, I use old cotton bed sheets from the thrift store. I prewash them and then cut them into pieces sized to fit in my steamer. I throw them in the wash along with my fabrics and reuse them for years. Plain newsprint works just fine, though I consider it more of a disposable material that has to be replenished. Be sure to avoid printed paper like old newspaper because last week's news could transfer onto your fabric!

YARN OR TWINE: Rather than securing your fabric in steaming cloths with tape that can come undone in the steam bath, tie it with some yarn or string. Don't bother with anything too pretty or precious; any thickness, brand, fiber content, and color will do. I have a cone of yarn from the clearance section at the fabric store that works fine for this purpose.

COOK-POT STEAMER: If you don't want to stand there ironing your fabric yardage for hours, it's easy to steam fabric in a cook pot on the stove. Use the largest pot you can find that you can designate specifically for dyeing. You'll also need a piece of household window screen. To build your own stove-top steaming rig, see Steam-Setting Your Fabric on page 103.

BOX STEAMER: I have a box steamer that is perfect for up to 5-yard (4.6 m) lengths of fabric. To put fabric into a box steamer, roll the fabric sandwich (the fabric layered between steaming cloths) around a pole. The pole is held at the box's ends by brackets that suspend it horizontally above the boiling water inside. Like the cook pot, the box steamer is heated on a stove top or hot plate, though the more than 3-foot-wide (.9 m) box steamer takes up both burners.

BULLET STEAMER: In high-volume production studios and educational centers, you'll see tall bullet steamers. Bullet steamers do not rely on stove-top burners but plug into an electrical outlet. Their steam heat source is a heater coil in a water reservoir in the base of the steamer, and their vertical sections come apart like boosters off a rocket. They are best for very big jobs and are very expensive. Unless you plan to invest in dyeing and steaming lots of fabric yardage and you are nimble on a ladder to climb above the steamer to drop the fabric tube down into it, stick with one of the other steamer options.

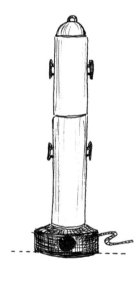

BRIEF OVERVIEW

Before printing with dyes on fabric, you'll need to make sure to have a few things ready. You'll need to prewash your fabric with Synthrapol to preshrink and scour it, removing any dirt, oil, chemicals, and other impurities that could interfere with the dyeing process. Plus you'll need to mix up a few stock solutions: for printing with dyes, you'll mix up dye stock solutions, urea water, and sodium alginate paste; to print with bleach, you'll need to mix monagum paste instead. Each solution is easy to mix and will make printing even faster because they'll be right there when you need them. See the helpful chart below and then move on!

COLORANT	SUBSTRATE FIBER	ACTIVATOR	AUXILIARY	THICKENER	STEAM-SET
MX FIBER REACTIVE DYES (TO PRINT)	Protein	Citric acid crystals	Urea, metaphos (optional)	Sodium alginate	Yes
MX FIBER REACTIVE DYES (TO PRINT)	Cellulose	Soda ash	Urea, metaphos (optional)	Sodium alginate	Yes
DISCHARGE PASTE	Protein, cellulose	None	None	None	Yes
THIOUREA DIOXIDE	Protein, cellulose	Soda ash	None	Sodium alginate	Yes
CHLORINE BLEACH	Cellulose	None	Neutralizers (hydrogen peroxide or antichlor)	Monagum	No
MX FIBER REACTIVE DYES (FOR IMMERSION)	Protein	Vinegar	None	None	No
MX FIBER REACTIVE DYES (FOR IMMERSION)	Cellulose	Soda ash	None	None	No

WASHING FABRIC WITH SYNTHRAPOL

As mentioned on page 92, Synthrapol is a special kind of detergent. It needs to be used on your fabric before and after the dyeing process itself for your finished fabric to look right and wear well.

YOU WILL NEED:

Your gloves and apron

Bucket

Fabric to be washed

Synthrapol

INSTRUCTIONS:

By hand

1 Wear your gloves! Soak the fabric in a small bucket in the sink in hot tap water with just a few drops of Synthrapol for about 5 minutes.

2 Rinse the detergent out of the fabric.

3 Wring it out and line dry or tumble in the dryer.

> **NOTE** *To wash excess dyes out of fabric, wash the same way and then rinse and keep changing the rinse water until it runs clear. You will see that acid-dyed silk rinses much more quickly than alkali-dyed cotton. Wring it out and line dry or tumble in the dryer.*

By machine

1 Wash fabric on hot cycle. If you have a full load going into a top-loading machine, you'll need about $1/4$ cup of Synthrapol. For a full load in a front loader, which is more efficient and uses less water, use $1/8$ cup of Synthrapol.

2 Line dry or tumble in the dryer. If you are concerned about the fibers in wool fabric felting in the machine, wash it gently by hand instead.

> **TIP** *Synthrapol is strong stuff, and a little goes a long way. If you will be doing a lot of hand washing, put some Synthrapol in a squeeze bottle to dispense a few drops at a time.*

MAKING STOCK SOLUTIONS AND PASTES

You can choose to keep your dyes in powder form in their jars and dissolve them as needed or to mix stock solutions by dissolving the dye in water, converting them from dry powder to liquid form. In this state, there are no fumes or tiny particles to become airborne and land on unsuspecting surfaces, including your lungs. So this means not having to don your respirator or dust mask every time you want to print with dye. Pastes are equally nice to have pre-mixed.

Making Dye Stock Solutions

Especially for screenprinting, you don't want your dye solution to be weak. Too much water will make it runny; likewise, not enough dye color and it will be pale. Clear plastic squeeze bottles from the beauty supply store are especially handy for holding stock solutions. You can mix one dye color per bottle and then intermix them from the bottles, squirt by squirt and drop by drop. Stock solutions have a shelf life of about six months to a year when stored away from heat and light. My recipe's ratio is simple and strong: 2 tablespoons of dye powder per 1 cup of water to yield rich, saturated colors. Feel free to multiply it as needed.

YOU WILL NEED:

Your gloves, apron, and respirator or dust mask

2 tablespoons MX dye powder in the jar

2-cup measuring cup

Room temperature water

Wire whisk

Funnel

Clear plastic squeeze bottle with tight-fitting lid and replaceable cap (one for each color)

Removable adhesive labels

Permanent marker for labeling

INSTRUCTIONS:

1 Put on your gloves, apron, and respirator or dust mask!

2 Scoop 2 level tablespoons of dye powder into a measuring cup. Be sure to replace the lid on the dye powder jar right away.

3 Add 1 cup of water to the dye powder. Whisk until all powder is completely dissolved.

4 Carefully pour the solution from the measuring cup through the funnel into the squeeze bottle.

5 Place the lid on the squeeze bottle.

6 Clearly label the bottle with the type of dye, color, and date mixed as shown.

7 Rinse your mixing and measuring tools and then repeat for each color solution you make.

8 When you are ready to use the dye stock solution, be sure to shake it well in case any dye has settled out of the solution.

Making a Urea Water Stock Solution

To make a quart of urea water to have on hand for dye printing, simply whisk the powder ingredients into hot water.

YOU WILL NEED:

Your apron and gloves

1-quart container with lid

Hot tap water

$1/2$ cup urea granules

1 teaspoon metaphos water softener, for hard water (optional)

INSTRUCTIONS:

1 Put on your apron and gloves.

2 Fill the quart container almost full with hot tap water.

3 Add urea granules.

4 Add metaphos, if desired.

5 Stir to dissolve the chemicals into solution.

Mixing Sodium Alginate Thickener Paste

For thickening dyes and thiox, use sodium alginate. This recipe makes 1 quart of thickener paste to have on hand for print-ing. The auxiliary chemicals urea and metaphos are specific to printing dyes, so if you are mixing paste to thicken thiox, you can omit them.

YOU WILL NEED:

Your apron and gloves

Hot tap water

Pitcher with lid and wire whisk

$^1/_2$ cup urea, for printing with dyes (optional)

1 teaspoon metaphos water softener, for printing with dyes (optional)

Sodium alginate, your choice of SH or F formulas (see page 92):

> For SH, you'll use about 4 to 6 tablespoons (about 1 tablespoon per cup)

> For F, you'll use about 12 to 15 tablespoons (about 3 tablespoons per cup)

 If you are getting ready to print with dye stock solutions and need to add some urea (and optional metaphos) into the mix, you can add it here.

INSTRUCTIONS:

1 Put on your apron and gloves.

2 Pour 1 quart of hot water in the pitcher.

3 Add $^1/_2$ cup urea granules and 1 teaspoon metaphos, if desired. Whisk well to dissolve. A

4 While rapidly whisking the water, slowly, slowly, slowly sprinkle in the sodium alginate powder, keeping an even, steady flow and consistency and avoiding the formation of stubborn clumps.

5 Let the mixture stand to even out its consistency for at least one hour, or overnight for the smoothest results, and then it's ready to mix with dyes for printing!

Making Monagum Paste for Thickening Bleach

Since sodium alginate cannot stand up to the oxidizing powers of bleach, mix up some monagum paste instead. Mix monagum the same way as alginate: whisk the powder into hot water and then let the mixture stand an hour to overnight to equalize their consistencies. This recipe is for 1 cup. To make a quart, use 8 tablespoons of monagum flakes per 1 quart water.

YOU WILL NEED:

Your apron and gloves

Pitcher with lid and wire whisk

1 cup hot tap water

2 tablespoons monagum flakes

INSTRUCTIONS:

1 Put on your apron and gloves.

2 Pour 1 cup hot water into pitcher.

3 Slowly sprinkle 2 tablespoons monagum flakes into the hot water while whisking.

4 Allow the mixture to stand about an hour to overnight to let the monagum paste achieve a smooth consistency. Then it's ready to thicken bleach for printing; jump ahead to page 102 to get started!

A

PRINTING WITH THICKENED DYES AND DISCHARGE AGENTS

Now that you've mixed all of your preliminary pastes and solutions, I'll show you how to put them together in simple recipes so they are fit to print. The printing part is pretty much the same as with inks, but then you'll need to steam the printed fabric and wash out the excess dyes.

Printing with Thickened Dyes

There's no such thing as an opaque dye formula, at least not in my world. Thickened dyes are transparent, so if you print a light color on a dark fabric, chances are it won't show up very well. So I recommend starting on some light-toned fabric so you can see what you are printing. This recipe will make 1 cup of thickened dye.

YOU WILL NEED:

Your apron and gloves

Urea water (if your thickener paste doesn't already have it in it)

Small 1- to 2-cup mixing container or measuring cup

Measuring spoons

MX dye powder (and respirator or dust mask) or MX dye stock solution (no mask necessary)

Activator: citric acid crystals for silk, soda ash for cotton

Wire whisk

Sodium alginate paste (page 98)

Pins

Prewashed fabric

Print surface (page 30)

Clean, dry, taped screen with stencil

Squeegee

INSTRUCTIONS:

1 Put on your apron and gloves. If you are working with powdered dyes, put on your respirator or dust mask.

2 If you're using dye powder, pour $1/4$ cup urea water into a small measuring cup. Add dye powder ($1/2$ teaspoon for pale color, 1 tablespoon for darker color, or double it for black). Stir until completely dissolved.

   For a dye stock solution, pour 1 tablespoon stock solution for pale color, 2 to 3 tablespoons for darker color, or 6 to 8 tablespoons for black into a small measuring cup.

3 Add 1 teaspoon activator. Stir with a wire whisk until completely dissolved.

4 Add sodium alginate thickener (with urea already in it) to make 1 cup and stir. Your thickened dye is ready to print!

5 Pin your fabric and print to your heart's delight (see Ready, Set, Print! on page 33).

6 Let the freshly printed fabric cure for about 24 hours. In the meantime, you can jump ahead to Steam-Setting Your Fabric on page 103 to see what's happening tomorrow.

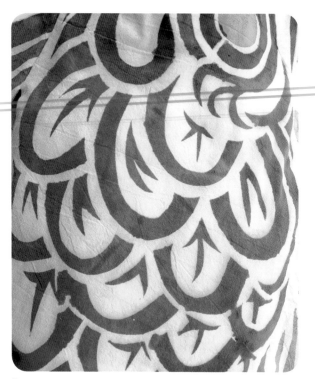

Fabric printed with thickened dye.

Once you are finished printing, you will need to give your fabric time to cure, steam-set it to complete the dye bonding process, and lastly, wash out all the chemicals to restore your fabric to its original feel. This is when the "real estate" on your print surface becomes very valuable. After printing, you need to let the dyes cure for at least overnight and up to 24 hours. Like Tom Petty said, "The waiting is the hardest part." Boy, was he right. I try to organize my day so I can print, leave the fabric on the table to cure overnight, and come back to steam-set it in the morning. If you can manage to pull your printed fabric off the print table while wet, move it to a sheet of plastic or a clothesline to get it out of the way. Wipe any dye off the print surface before pinning new fabric to print.

Printing with Discharge Paste or Thiox

Since discharge paste is already thickened and activated to print straight out of the jar, there is no preliminary mixing involved. This means that you can jump right down to step 6.

Thiox, on the other hand, must be thickened and activated to print. So if you haven't already mixed up a batch of sodium alginate, be sure to do it before mixing your thiox for printing. See Mixing Sodium Alginate Thickener Paste on page 98, leaving out the urea and metaphos; those auxiliaries are only used with dyes and are unnecessary for thiox. Mix thiox right before you start printing. And don't mix more than you need for the day. Once it is activated and thickened it is highly reactive; it lasts for maybe 12 hours and then loses its potency.

▌ Fabric printed with discharge paste.

▌ Fabric printed with thiox.

YOU WILL NEED:

Your apron, gloves, and respirator with vapor cartridges

2-cup mixing container

Hot water

1 teaspoon thiourea dioxide (thiox)

2 teaspoons soda ash

Wire whisk

Sodium alginate paste (page 98)

Pins

Prewashed fabric

Print surface (page 30)

Clean, dry, taped screen with stencil

Squeegee

Steaming cloths or blank newsprint (see page 94)

Steamer of your choice (see page 94)

Synthrapol

INSTRUCTIONS:

1 Put on your apron, gloves, and respirator.

2 In your mixing container, pour ¼ cup hot water.

3 Add 1 teaspoon thiox powder and 2 teaspoons soda ash. Stir with a wire whisk until dissolved.

4 Add sodium alginate paste to make 1 cup and stir to blend.

5 Allow the consistency to even out for about 15 minutes to 1 hour, and then it is ready to print!

6 Pin your fabric and print to your heart's delight (see Ready, Set, Print on page 33).

7 After printing, allow the printed areas to dry just enough so that they don't smear when rolled for steaming.

8 Sandwich the printed fabric between steaming cloths or newsprint and place in the steamer over boiling water. Steam for 15 to 20 minutes (for instructions, jump ahead to Steam-Setting Your Fabric on page 103).

9 Take the steamed fabric outside to unwrap it; there will be a lot of stinky, steamy fumes as you open it up!

10 Thoroughly wash out the fabric in hot water with Synthrapol. Wring it out and line dry or tumble in the dryer.

Printing with Thickened Chlorine Bleach

Bleach is highly reactive and works very quickly, even breaking down the monagum paste that thickens it within a few hours. Once you print it on the fabric, it can react within seconds or more slowly—in minutes—so you want to be ready for it. Mix the bleach and thickener together only after everything else is ready to print, including your neutralizing agents (hydrogen peroxide 3% or an antichlor bath). Then unleash the beast!

YOU WILL NEED:

Print surface (page 30)

Pins

Prewashed fabric

Clean, dry, and taped screen with stencil

Squeegee

1 cup monagum paste (see recipe on page 98)

2-cup mixing container

2 tablespoons chlorine bleach

Wire whisk

Hydrogen peroxide 3% (approximately 1 16-ounce bottle per yard of printed fabric) *or* 1 teaspoon antichlor plus 2 gallons warm water

Synthrapol

Hot water

▌ Fabric printed with thickened chlorine bleach.

INSTRUCTIONS:

1 Get ready to print: pin down your fabrics on your work surface with your screen and squeegee nearby.

2 Pour 1 cup monagum paste in your mixing container.

3 Add 2 tablespoons chlorine bleach and whisk to mix.

4 Pin your fabric and print to your heart's delight! Bleach solution is very stinky and even burns your eyes, so work quickly to get it over with. You will see the printed areas change color momentarily or within 20 minutes; it can vary widely.

 It is not necessary to steam-set the fabric to activate bleach. Bleach works just fine on its own, thank you very much!

5 Once the desired color change is achieved, neutralize it right away! You can do this one of two ways:

(a) Pour hydrogen peroxide straight from the bottle right onto the printed fabric. Then rinse it several times in hot water.

(b) Mix a bath of 1 teaspoon antichlor and 2 gallons warm water in a large container and add the fabric right from the print table. Soak the printed fabric for 5 minutes.

6 With bleach, it's better to overdo the rinsing than not rinse enough, since residual bleach in fabric can continue to wear and degrade the fabric long after rinsing. I recommend changing the rinse water at least three or four times.

7 Thoroughly wash out the fabric in hot water with Synthrapol. Wring it out and line dry or tumble in the dryer.

Immersion Dyeing Cotton Fabric

To dye cotton and other plant-based fibers, we've got to rearrange the steps just slightly. You will need the same equipment, but instead of vinegar, you'll use a soda ash as the activator. Dyeing plant fibers is not as efficient as dyeing silk, so I find that I need more dye to achieve the same shade of color: for every teaspoon of dye I use on a yard of silk, I use a tablespoon of dye for a yard of cotton. The bath does not run clear as the dye migrates into the cellulose fibers, so you cannot use it as a visual gauge for absorption—just give it time! I usually allow it to sit at least overnight or up to 24 hours in the bath before washing it. After a while, the dye molecules start bonding with the water molecules instead of the fabric, so you cannot reuse an alkaline bath. Just neutralize it with a little vinegar and discard it.

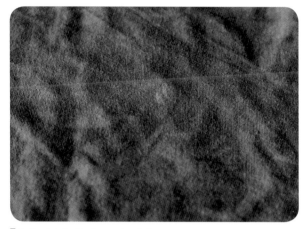

 Cotton fabric after immersion dyeing.

YOU WILL NEED:

Your apron and gloves

Respirator or dust mask (if using dye powder)

1- to 3-gallon bucket

Room temperature tap water

2 small mixing containers

Measuring spoons

Approximately 1 tablespoon MX dye powder (with respirator or dust mask) or 3 tablespoons MX dye stock solution (mask not necessary)

1 to 2 yards (.9 to 1.8 m) prewashed cotton fabric

1 tablespoon soda ash (activator)

Synthrapol

Hot water

INSTRUCTIONS:

1 Put on you apron or gloves. If you are working with dye powder, put on your respirator or dust mask.

2 Fill your bucket with enough water to completely immerse fabric, but don't add the fabric yet.

3 Fill a separate small container about half full of water.

4 Add 1 tablespoon dye powder or 3 tablespoons stock solution; use a smaller amount for pale colors, more for darker colors, or double it for black. You may add multiple colors and mix colors in the small container at this point if you like.

5 Stir until the dye is completely dissolved. This can take several minutes of stirring!

6 Pour the dye solution into the bucket.

7 Add the fabric and stir to get the dye to intermingle with the fabric. Let stand for 15 minutes. Cellulose fibers are a bit more shy than silk! They need that time to get settled in with the dye before adding the activator. Weird but true!

8 After 15 minutes, fill a separate small mixing container about half full of water. Add 1 tablespoon soda ash and dissolve completely.

9 Add the dissolved soda ash solution to the dye bath and stir well. Wear your gloves and turn the fabric around in the bath to ensure the activator has reached all over.

10 Let it soak at least overnight and up to 24 hours.

11 Thoroughly wash out the fabric in hot water with Synthrapol, wring it out, and line dry or tumble in the dryer.

Now you've got your very own gorgeous hand-dyed fabric to print and layer however you like! If you'd like to throw it in another alkaline dye bath, simply repeat, and you can save a step and do it before the final washing.

CHAPTER 7

THE PROJECTS

You've seen all there is to see, and maybe you've even pulled a few prints. But now you're ready for ideas, inspiration, and all sorts of projects to put techniques into practice! In this section you'll see a wide variety of motifs printed on a wide variety of fabrics. There are even a couple of projects designed to use up those pretty printed scraps. I hope you find something that speaks to you. And of course, feel free to mix-and-match ideas to your heart's content.

PUFFY CLOUD PILLOWS

Make your favorite sitting spot a little dreamier with washable pillowcases to cover store-bought inserts. Drawing fluid is ideal for painting the dots of this cloud pattern. And if you print with puff extender like I did, the clouds will actually be puffy! I've made two pillows, a little one with big dots and a big one with little dots, but you can mix sizes and patterns however you'd like. Note that this project assumes you know how to sew a zipper—if you don't know how, refer to your favorite sewing book, look for a video online, or rework it to use buttons instead!

YOU WILL NEED:

Printing surface (page 30)

Templates: (page 148)

Clean, dry, and taped 12 x 16-inch (30.5 x 40.6 cm) screen

Scotch tape

Drawing fluid

Small, flat-tipped paintbrush

Screen filler

Squeegee

Cold water and spray nozzle

Pins

Prewashed blue woven fabric

Puff base extender: about 8 ounces per pillow

Color concentrate to tint the puff base extender (optional)

Kraft paper

Iron and ironing surface

Fabric shears

Sewing machine with universal needle

Sewing thread to match the fabric

Zipper at least 2 inches (5.1 cm) shorter than width of pillow

Embroidery floss in an accent color

Embroidery needle

INSTRUCTIONS:

1   Copy the templates on page 148 and make sure they fit your print window. If you prefer to paint fewer dots, feel free to use a smaller segment of the template.

2   Tape the template inside your screen, face down, and paint all the dot cutouts on the outside of the screen with drawing fluid (for a refresher on drawing fluid, see page 48). To achieve a mosaic effect, use a square-tipped brush and paint as shown. **A** Once the fluid is dry, apply the screen filler with a squeegee to the same side of the screen that you applied the drawing fluid. Allow the screen filler to dry completely (overnight if possible) and then spray out the drawing fluid with cold water.

3   Pin down the blue fabric. I used the puff extender right out of the jar; it turns opaque white. If you'd like to color it, mix in a few drops of color concentrate. Print the clouds in an implied repeat, turning and tumbling the screen.

4   Allow the prints to dry completely and then fill in with more prints to build bigger motifs as shown.

5   When your prints are completely dry, layer the fabric between kraft paper on your ironing surface and, using a dry iron, press the fabric at the hottest setting your fabric can stand. Within a few minutes, the heat activates the base extender, and it will puff up.

A

6 Cut two squares from your fabric for each pillow to the same dimensions as your pillow inserts. (Mine were 18 inches square [45.7 cm] and 22 inches square [55.9 cm].) Pick one panel for the front and one for the back. Cut the back panel into two equally sized pieces. Insert the zipper to join the two pieces together again, centering the zipper on the seam and sewing the seam all the way to the ends.

7 With right sides together, sew the two squares together to make the pillowcase. Unzip the opening in the back, turn it right side out, and put the insert in the pillowcase.

8 On the front panel, hand stitch the outlines around the cloud motifs in embroidery floss and knot off. I used a basic running stitch. Puffy, dreamy goodness! **B**

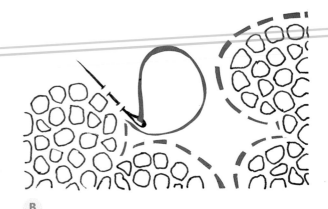

B

BUTTERFLY CHAIR COVER

I love the lines of this midcentury modern icon, and printing a fresh cover is an affordable and easy way to give it a new look. I added some texture and history by printing paraffin wax rubbings of my great-grandfather's old license plate and masked off a strip of unprinted area for visual interest.

YOU WILL NEED:

Printing surface (page 30)

Clean, dry, and taped 12 x 16-inch
    (30.5 x 40.6 cm) screen

License plate

Paraffin wax

Sheet of acetate or Mylar

Scotch tape

Fine-point permanent marker

Craft knife

Cutting mat

Masking tape

Thickened and freshly activated thiox
    print paste (page 101)

Squeegee

Prewashed cotton butterfly-chair cover

Steamer and steaming cloths (page 103)

Synthrapol

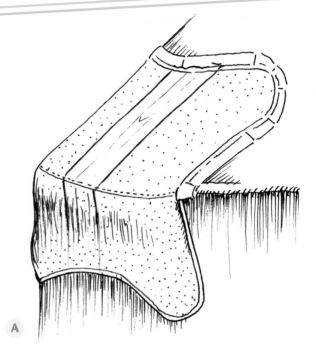

INSTRUCTIONS:

1   Place the screen on the license plate and make a tex-
    ture rubbing with paraffin wax. (For a refresher, see
    page 41.)

2   Place the acetate over the rubbing and tape it in place
    with a little Scotch tape. Trace around the numbers,
    letters, and other details with a fine-point marker,
    leaving about ¼-inch (.6 cm) clearance around them.
    Remove the acetate from the screen and cut out the
    areas to print. Then place the acetate back on the
    screen and tape around the perimeter with masking
    tape for printing.

3   Mask the binding of the chair cover as well as
    the vertical band with masking tape. Due to the
    three-dimensional, concave shape of the chair cover,
    I find it easiest to print one corner at a time, allowing
    the other three sides to hang off the table. A

4   Print the thiox paste onto the chair cover, tumbling
    and overlapping the print.

5   Once you've finished printing, let the thiox dry,
    remove the masking tape, roll the cover in steaming
    cloths and steam for 20 minutes (see page 103). Wash
    the cover in Synthrapol, dry it, and put it on your chair
    frame. What was old is new again!

TRAVEL BACKGAMMON SET

Backgammon reminds me of J. D. Weed Antiques, where I played backgammon with customers in the hopes they would have so much fun on the handmade backgammon tables they would buy one, or some other expensive antiques. This game-board stencil is very simple so you can quickly cut it out of acetate or Mylar, print in two colors, and then assemble the board—complete with a pocket to hold your game pieces!

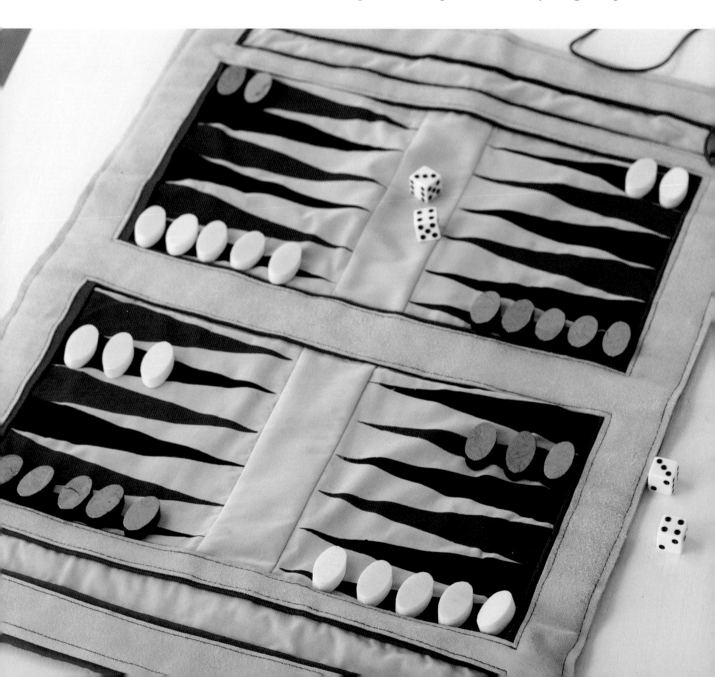

YOU WILL NEED:

Printing surface (page 30)

Templates: pages 149 and 150

Piece of Mylar or acetate slightly larger than the screen's print window

Craft knife

Cutting mat

Scotch tape

Clean, dry, and taped 12 x 16-inch (30.5 x 40.6 cm) screen

T-square with ruler

Grease pencils in black and red

12 x 45-inch (30.5 x 114.3 cm) piece of prewashed aqua blue cotton fabric

Opaque textile ink: black and red

Squeegee

Iron and ironing board for heat-setting

Fabric shears

Pins

Sewing machine with universal needle and leather needle

Sewing thread in light neutral color and in red

1 yard (.9 m) of red acrylic felt

4 square feet (.4 square meters) of pale gray suede

Masking tape

Pencil

Hand-sewing needle

1 yard (.9 m) of red cord

Red embroidery floss

1 shank button, 1 inch (2.5 cm) in diameter

30 game pieces, 15 each in 2 colors (I used oval ceramic tiles in gray and white)

4 dice

INSTRUCTIONS:

1   Copy and center the Backgammon Triangles templates on the acetate and cut out the triangles. Tape the acetate stencil to the print side of the print window, making sure the baseline of the triangles is parallel to the screen frame. (For a refresher on stencils, see page 45).

2   Mark four 10-inch (25.4 cm) horizontal increments on the T-square in black grease pencil. This will leave enough clearance around each game-board section for sewing. Then make red marks 1 ¼ inches (3.2 cm) to the right of the black marks.

3   Aligning the X on the screen with the black marks, print four repeats in a row in black. **A** Let the ink dry completely. Align the X on the screen with the red marks and print four repeats in red as shown. **B** Let the ink dry completely and heat-set your fresh prints.

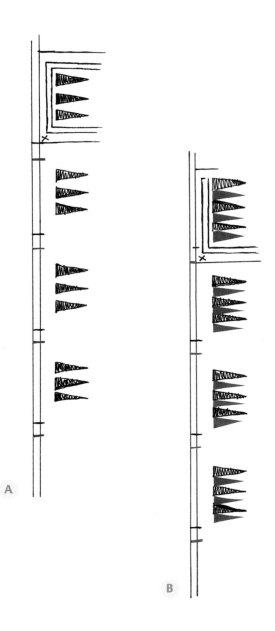

A

B

4 Trim each printed fabric panel to 8 x 7 inches
   (20.3 x 17.8 cm), leaving a ¼-inch (.6 cm) allowance
   above the tips of the triangles. Cut the following
   pieces from cotton to complete the playing board:

   (a) Four 8 x 7-inch (20.3 x 17.8 cm) panels with
       triangles

   (b) Two 2 ½ x 8-inch (6.4 x 20.3 cm) pieces
       (to space between two triangle fields)

   (c) One 2 x 16-inch (5.1 x 40.6 cm) center bar piece

   (d) Two 3 x 16-inch (7.6 x 40.6 cm) end zones

   To sew the pieces together, carefully align one triangle
   field to one center, then attach the other triangle field,
   triangle tips pointing to the center. **C** Repeat. Sew
   each to the center bar, add the end zones, and iron all
   seams flat. **D**

5 Place the resized Game Board Frame template on the
   red felt. Cut the felt along the dotted lines with the
   craft knife and ruler. Cut another piece of felt along
   the outside for a solid piece.

6 Carefully align and layer the solid piece of felt, the
   playing board, and the windowed felt. Pin in place.
   Sew through all three layers with at least ½-inch
   (1.3 cm) allowance around the windows.

7 Cut one piece of suede along the solid lines of the
   template and another along the outside for a solid
   piece, which will be the outer cover; set the outer
   cover aside for now. Layer the windowed suede with
   the game board and use masking tape to hold it in
   place. With the leather needle, sew through all layers
   around the windows with no more than a ¼-inch
   (.6 cm) seam allowance.

8 To make the pocket for the game pieces, cut a piece
   of felt the height of the framed board (mine was
   17 inches [43.2 cm]) by 8 inches (20.3 cm). Fold it in
   half lengthwise. Sew one side to the back of the
   framed game board and the other side to the inside
   of the suede outer cover as shown. **E**

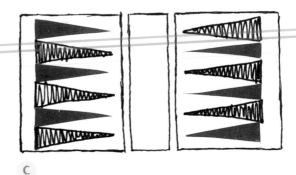

C

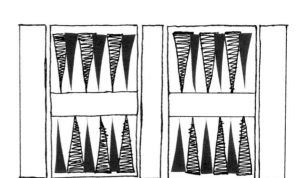

D

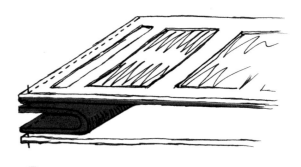

E

F

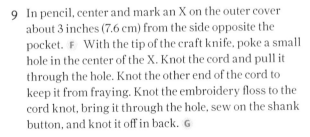

G

9   In pencil, center and mark an X on the outer cover about 3 inches (7.6 cm) from the side opposite the pocket. **F** With the tip of the craft knife, poke a small hole in the center of the X. Knot the cord and pull it through the hole. Knot the other end of the cord to keep it from fraying. Knot the embroidery floss to the cord knot, bring it through the hole, sew on the shank button, and knot it off in back. **G**

10 Use masking tape to tape the game board to the outer cover and sew together on the three remaining sides, leaving the pocket side open. Trim your threads, pack up your game pieces, and go find an opponent to play on your new board!

HONEYCOMB FOLDING SCREEN

Last year, I became a beekeeper. Whenever I opened the hive, I marveled at the combs the bees were building and filling with nectar. When I wanted to create the same pattern for this folding screen, I chose to cut the honeycomb shape out of contact paper and add texture with a rubbing of the ball-head pins sticking out of my pincushion. This process reminded me how fun and immediate low-tech printing can be!

YOU WILL NEED:

Printing surface (page 30)

Clean, dry, and taped 20 x 24-inch
   (50.8 x 61 cm) screen

Paraffin wax

Ball-head pins and pincushion (or your choice of
   textured surface)

Template: page 151

Contact paper

Craft knife

Cutting mat

Kraft paper

Apron, gloves, and respirator

Luan plywood or foam core cut to fit in the
   folding screen's slide-in compartments
   (my screen needed 3 of them)

Metal folding screen frame with slide-in compartments
   (I googled metal folding screen)

Spray adhesive

2 yards (1.8 m) of prewashed lightweight cotton
   muslin to completely cover the panels

Bone folder or spoon

Textile ink: golden yellow and silver

Transparent base extender

Acrylic ink: turquoise

Small cup for acrylic wash

Small 1-inch (2.5 cm) paintbrush

INSTRUCTIONS:

1 Make texture rubbings on your screens with the paraffin wax (see page 41 for a refresher on this
   technique). I made a rubbing of the pinheads sticking
   out of my pincushion.

2 Resize the template to fit your print windows, trace
   the stencil onto the contact paper, and cut out the honeycomb motif. Adhere the stencil to the screen (see
   page 44 for instructions). Don't throw away the
   hexagon shapes you cut out; you'll put them to use
   when you print the silver layer.

3 Put down kraft paper to protect your print surface.
   Put on your apron, gloves, and respirator. Lay out the
   plywood panels together in the configuration that
   they will hang in the screen and spray them gener-
   ously with spray adhesive.

4 Lay the muslin on the wood panels and stretch it taut
   and flat to entirely cover the wood. Burnish the surface with a bone folder so it is completely flat. Trim off
   the excess fabric with the craft knife and slice
   between the plywood panels to separate them. Once
   the air has cleared, you can remove your respirator.

5 Mix about ½ cup of golden yellow textile ink with
   ½ cup transparent extender base and print the honeycomb in an implied repeat pattern (page 70).

6 Grab those shelf-paper hexagons you set aside in
   step 2 and cut them to make them about an inch
   (2.5 cm) smaller. Peel a few of the small hexagonal
   pieces of contact paper and stick them within the
   honeycomb windows on your screen. Mix about
   ½ cup of silver ink into the transparent yellow and
   continue printing the honeycomb in an implied
   repeat pattern. A

7 Water down the acrylic ink to make a light aqua wash.
   Paint the areas between the prints, leaving at least a
   ¼- to ½-inch (.6 to 1.3 cm) clearance. Allow them to
   dry completely, then slide the panels into the frame. I
   can almost hear the bees buzzing in the comb! B

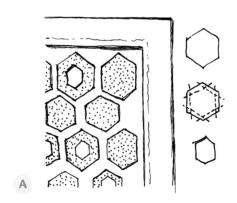

BICYCLE BEACH TOTE

It's funny when the stuff you received a long time ago suddenly becomes cool again. My parents gave me a 10-speed bike (originally lavender and white) for my 13th birthday back in the 1980s, and now it is purely decorative, suspended from the ceiling of my studio. I found the perfect bag on which to print it—brand new but so '80s retro.

YOU WILL NEED:

Template: page 148

Copier or copy shop and acetate to make 2 transparencies

Photo emulsion

12 x 16-inch (30.5 x 40.6 cm) clean, dry, and taped screen

Setup for photo emulsion: darkroom, exposure unit, spray sink (page 52)

Tape measure

Canvas tote bag

Pins

T-shirt insert (page 29)

Mixing container and spoon

Textile ink: opaque red-orange (red + yellow)

Squeegee

Hair dryer

Iron and ironing board for heat-setting

INSTRUCTIONS:

1   Resize the template to fit your print window and make a two-ply transparency on acetate (page 58, Step 9). Follow the instructions for photo emulsion (page 61) to coat, expose, and spray out your screen.

2   Measure the circumference of the beach tote and use the number to figure how many times you can fit the bicycle image in a continuous repeat. It can be overlapping or spaced apart. Use the transparency to eyeball the image placement, and pin to mark the sides of the image on the bag to help guide your screen placement when printing.

3   Insert the T-shirt insert inside the tote and pin it down if necessary. Mix your inks; print the first bicycle. Dry it with a hair dryer and reposition the bag to print the next bicycle; repeat until your last bicycle print reaches the first. After the ink on the final bicycle is dry, iron the bag to heat-set your fresh prints. Totally awesome!

FERRIS WHEEL SKIRT

Straight from my lifelong visual vocabulary is my Ferris wheel, originally cut from paper. Growing up in rural Indiana, I have fond childhood memories of the Lake County Fair and wackier teenage memories of running the carnival rides at a decrepit little amusement park in town. The A-line cut of the skirt is simple, but the reverse appliqué areas within the structure of the Ferris wheel are intricately detailed.

YOU WILL NEED:

Printing surface (page 30)

Template: page 152

Copier or copy shop and acetate to make 2 transparencies

Clean, dry, and taped 20 x 24-inch (50.8 x 61 cm) screen

Photo emulsion

Setup for photo emulsion: darkroom, exposure unit, spray sink (page 52)

Dressmaker's measuring tape

2 yards (1.8 m) of 30-inch-wide (76.2 cm) brown kraft paper

Long ruler or yardstick

Fabric shears

Fine-point permanent marker for drawing dress pattern

Prewashed fuchsia cotton or bamboo jersey knit fabric

Prewashed chartreuse cotton or bamboo jersey knit fabric

Pins

Textile ink: opaque violet

Squeegee

Iron and ironing surface for heat-setting

Sewing machine with universal needle

Darning foot and free-motion capability (optional but recommended)

Serger (optional)

Red and black sewing thread

Fabric scraps (I used black jersey)

 Though it's made of jersey knit, you don't need a serger to sew this skirt. I have written the instructions for a regular sewing machine. If you have a serger, feel free to use it; I would construct it with a four-thread mock safety stitch and roll the hems.

INSTRUCTIONS:

1   Since this is a larger image stencil (13 x 15 inches [33 x 38.1 cm]), you may need to take it to a copy shop to have it enlarged, or just enlarge it yourself but to a more managable size. Make a two-ply transparency on acetate (see page 58, Step 9). Follow the instructions for photo emulsion to coat, expose, and spray out your screen (see page 61).

2   Make your skirt pattern. Use the measuring tape to measure your waist where you would like the waistband to sit; measure the widest part of your hips. Measure the vertical distance between them. Draw the skirt pattern with a fine-point marker onto the kraft paper according to your measurements. Draw your preferred skirt length; mine was 24 inches (61 cm). Use a yardstick to draw the side seam from the hip to the hemline as straight as possible, no curving in or out, which will distort the side seam.

Here is a rough size guide I use for stretch fabrics:

	X-SMALL	SMALL	MEDIUM	LARGE	X-LARGE
SIZE	0–2	4–6	8–10	12–14	16–18
WAIST	25" (63.5 cm)	28" (71.1 cm)	31" (78.7 cm)	34" (86.3 cm)	37" (94 cm)
CUT WAIST FROM FOLD	6 ¼" (15.9 cm)	7" (17.8 cm)	7 ¾" (19.7 cm)	8 ½" (21.6 cm)	9 ¼" (23.5 cm)
HIP	34" (86.3 cm)	38" (96.5 cm)	41" (104.1 cm)	44" (111.8 cm)	48" (121.9 cm)
CUT HIP FROM FOLD	8 ½" (21.6 cm)	9 ½" (24.1 cm)	10 ¼" (26 cm)	11" (27.9 cm)	12" (30.5 cm)

The formula is simple, really. The overall waist and hip measurements are listed. Since you will be cutting two identical skirt panels (front and back) folded in half, the distance from the fold is ¼ of the measurement. If your measurements vary a bit from the standards, it's fine to pull numbers from one or the other. See the example. **A**

Once you've made your kraft-paper pattern, you can use the pattern to determine how much fabric you need, which depends upon the width of your fabric. The people at the fabric store ought to be able to help you figure out the correct yardage you need for your particular size and length. You will need enough to cut two panels out of fuchsia jersey (face fabric) and two out of chartreuse jersey (lining), each on the fold as shown. Cut out the four skirt panels according to the panel on the fold, two from fuchsia and two from chartreuse.

3 Pin down the two fuchsia skirt pieces on the print surface and print one Ferris wheel on each near the side seam where they will be next to each other as shown. **B** For a refresher on printing, see page 33. Dry it completely and heat-set your fresh prints.

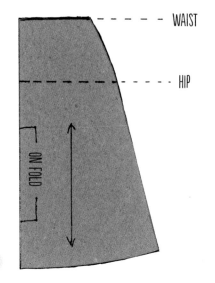

A

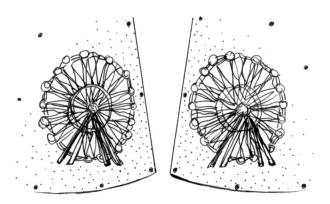

B

4   Layer each fuchsia skirt panel with each chartreuse skirt panel, each with right side facing upward. Pin the layers together every few inches among and around the Ferris wheel print. For the next two steps, you will treat the two layers of fabric like one.

5   Thread the sewing machine with red thread and stitch along the edges of the negative spaces within the Ferris wheel print so you can trim away what's inside. You can let the machine drive, but if your machine has free-motion capability, I highly recommend using it for this intricate design! It will save you lots of time. Likewise, don't cut and restart your sewing thread as you jump from one stitched area to the next; you'll cut those later. Pull the pins as you stitch.

6   Pinch apart the two layers of negative space within the Ferris wheel and carefully snip at only the fuchsia layer to cut out a window to expose the chartreuse layer behind. Now you can also trim the threads running from window to window as you go.

7   With right sides together, sew the front and back skirt panels at the side seams. C

8   To make the waistband, cut a long piece of black jersey 4 inches (10.2 cm) wide. Subtract 1 inch (2.5 cm) from your waist measurement to use as the length. For example, a medium waistband would measure 4 x 30 inches (10.3 x 76.2 cm). D With right sides together, sew the short ends of the waistband piece together to make a closed loop. E Fold the waistband in half lengthwise, right sides together. F Pin to the skirt as shown, matching the waistband seam with one side seam. Sew the waistband to the skirt with a mock overlock stitch, which is stretchable so you can get the skirt off and on! G

9   Leave the fuchsia skirt hem edge raw, but make it more intentional and stable by stitching a narrow zigzag using red thread within ¼ inch (.6 cm) of the edge. Repeat to separately stitch the chartreuse layer with black thread. Trim your threads. Your new skirt is ready for a fun night out!

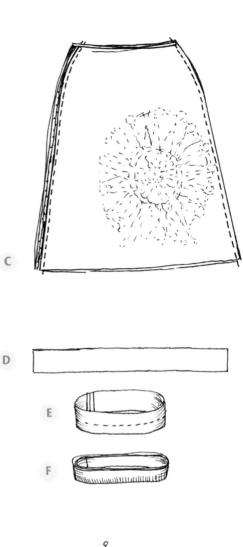

C

D

E

F

G

OGEE CURTAINS

Transform some store-bought curtains with an exotic ogee in a sophisticated half-drop repeat. I cut the original ogee motif out of black construction paper while sitting in my tent at a craft fair somewhere. With its not-quite symmetrical shape, it's very forgiving if you goof a little here and there on your registration. I even printed a row or two upside down, but that's our little secret!

YOU WILL NEED:

Printing surface with measuring tape (pages 30 and 72)

Template: page 155

Copier or copy shop and acetate to make transparencies

Clean, dry, and taped 12 x 16-inch (30.5 x 40.6 cm) screen

Photo emulsion

Setup for photo emulsion: darkroom, exposure unit, spray sink (page 52)

Pins

2 prewashed 84-inch-long (213.4 cm) white curtains

Masking tape

Scrap paper (optional)

T-square with ruler

Grease pencil

Mixing containers and spoons

Textile ink in 2 colors, about 1 cup of each color per curtain (I used red and black to make dark plum, and red and yellow to make orange)

Squeegee

Hair dryer

Iron and ironing board for heat setting

INSTRUCTIONS:

1   Resize the template to fit your print window and make a two-ply transparency on acetate (page 58, Step 9). Follow the instructions for photo emulsion to coat, expose, and spray out your screen (page 61).

2   Pin the curtain(s) down to the print table and mask off the top ties and bottom hems with tape and the optional scrap paper. If you have the luxury of a table big enough to print both curtains at the same time, lucky you! If you are printing one at a time like I did, trace the outline of the first curtain onto the table with a grease pencil. This will help you align the second one in the same position to match them.

3   Make your printing marks (see page 81). To center the design horizontally, center the screen at the top of the curtain and place your horizontal increment marks out from there.

4   Mix your textile ink and refer to the half-drop instructions on page 81 to print. Print in half-drop repeat sequence, drying all prints with a hair dryer between printing sessions. Start with orange in the top left corner for the first session, then orange again one step below to form vertical columns in the second session. Then print the third session in dark plum a half-step down and one over from the first and finally the fourth session in dark plum to fill in the remaining vertical columns.

5   Dry all prints completely, remove the masking tape, and pull all pins. To print another curtain, carefully place it in the same position as the first (within the area with the grease pencil from step 2), and print using the same marks and sequence as the first. Heat-set your fresh prints (page 35) and hang your curtains.

MEADOW CARDIGAN

The chartreuse color of this cardigan reminds me of a clearing in the woods where I trail run with my dog Rosco. On one run, I made sure to bring my phone to photograph the wild joe-pye weed growing along the trail in the meadow. To turn a simple store-bought cardigan into a wearable landscape, I overlapped and wrapped the pattern around to the back and the sleeve. I added to its depth and dimension by printing the image in three shades and hand stitching a few details.

YOU WILL NEED:

Printing surface (page 30)

Template: page 154

Copier or copy shop and acetate to make 2 transparencies

Clean, dry, and taped 12 x 16-inch (30.5 x 40.6 cm) screen

Photo emulsion

Setup for photo emulsion: darkroom, exposure unit, spray sink (page 52)

Pins

Cardigan

Kraft paper

Mixing containers and spoons

Opaque textile ink: blue, white, and black

    light blue = blue + white

    blue-gray = blue + white + black

    dark blue = blue + black

Squeegee

Hair dryer (optional)

Iron and ironing board for heat-setting

Embroidery floss in coordinating colors like turquoise, gray, or white

Embroidery needle

Fabric snips

INSTRUCTIONS:

1 Resize the template to fit your print window and make a two-ply transparency on acetate. Follow the instructions for photo emulsion to coat, expose, and spray out your screen (page 61).

2 Pin the cardigan to your print surface and mask with kraft paper as shown. **A** Mix the shades of textile ink you want to print. Print multiple motifs on the sleeve and buttonhole side of the cardigan, varying the three colors on the squeegee and letting them dry completely (using a hair dryer if desired) before moving on.

3 Re-pin and mask the cardigan as shown, masking the bottom binding with scrap paper. **B** Continue printing to wrap the design around to the back of the cardigan and let that side dry completely. Heat-set your fresh prints (page 35).

4 Hand embroider a few stalks and details if you'd like. I used a simple running stitch and backstitch on mine.

TOUGH GUY BABY JUMPERS

My gearhead dad is the original inspiration for printing cars on baby clothes, and the muscle car template is my dad's 1967 Buick Skylark. The other images used for this project are my Lonely Robot illustration and images from wonderful collections of copyright-free clip art (see Resources, page 158). Make your detailed screens with photo emulsion and cut the low-tech silhouette stencil out of contact paper.

YOU WILL NEED:

Printing surface (page 30)

Templates: page 153

Copier or copy shop and acetate to make 2 transparencies

2 clean, dry, and taped 12 x 16-inch (30.5 x 40.6 cm) screens: 1 for the photo emulsion stencil from the template, 1 for the low-tech silhouette stencil

Photo emulsion

Setup for photo emulsion: darkroom, exposure unit, spray sink (page 52)

Contact paper

Fine-point permanent marker

Craft knife

Cutting mat

Kraft paper

At least 1 pack of one-piece infant jumpers

Pins

Mixing containers and spoons

Opaque textile inks: see color table below

Squeegee

Hair dryer

Small paintbrush for touch-ups and details

Iron and ironing board for heat-setting

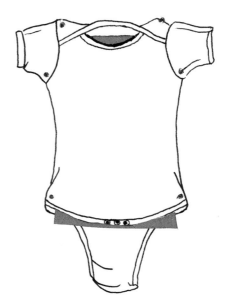

INSTRUCTIONS:

1   For the detailed image you're going to print, resize the template of your choice to fit your print window and make a two-ply transparency on acetate (page 58, Step 9). Follow the instructions for photo emulsion to coat, expose, and spray out one screen (see page 61).

2   For the silhouette layer, you will now need a sheet of contact paper a little larger than your print window and the other screen. Start by tracing the outside contours of the transparency from step 1 onto the peel-away gridded paper side of the contact paper. Cut out the traced silhouette and discard it or save it for another project. Peel the paper backing and adhere the contact paper to the print side of the blank screen. If there are any details you don't want to print for this layer, like the robot's eyes and heart cavity (see page 134), you can cut out those shapes and stick them on this screen as well.

3   Slip a piece of scrap kraft paper inside the garment and pin as shown. Print the silhouette layer from step 2 first and allow it to dry it completely (speed things along with a hair dryer). You can touch up or add small details with a paintbrush if you'd like. Dry and heat-set your prints (see page 35).

NOTE *Since one-piece baby jumpers come in a variety of whites, colors, and prints, feel free to get a selection. I immersion dyed the ones shown here, and you can, too! Refer to page 105 for immersion-dyeing cotton instructions.*

TEMPLATE	FABRIC	SILHOUETTE PRINT	DETAILED IMAGE PRINT
Muscle Car	white	silver + turquoise	black
Lincoln	brown	orange	black
Sparrow	red	gold	black
Lonely Robot	blue	silver	black, paint heart red

PRIZE WINNER PET BED

My friend Erin has six or seven cats and gives them prizes for Cat of the Day, Cat of the Month, and of course, Cat of the Year. Everyone's a winner! Inspired by Erin's awards, I made my dog Sesame a pet bed with her very own prize ribbon. Since the brick layout of this print pattern has lots of room between each repeat, you can print it all in one session. The finished size is 35 x 30 x 5 inches (88.9 x 76.2 x 12.7 cm).

Printing surface with measuring tape (pages 30 and 72)

Template: page 156

Clean, dry, and taped 12 x 16-inch (30.5 x 40.6 cm) screen with Prize Winner Ribbon stencil (5 x 10 ¼ inches [12.7 x 26 cm]) applied with photo emulsion (page 61)

T-square with ruler

Grease pencil in two colors

Pins

2 ½ yards (2.3 m) of 45-inch-wide (114.3 cm) navy blue cotton sheeting

Squeegee

Thickened bleach paste (page 102)

2 or 3 bottles of hydrogen peroxide 3%

Synthrapol

Fabric shears

Sewing machine with zipper foot (I used Bernina #4) and universal needle

Navy blue sewing thread

9 continuous yards (8.2 m) or four 2 ½-yard (2.3 m) packages of white piping

Iron and ironing board

1 yard (.9 m) of 1-inch-wide (2.5 cm) sewable Velcro

Stuffing for the bed (I used an old egg-crate foam mattress pad and cut it into four 35 x 30-inch (88.9 x 76.2 cm) pieces to layer together, but you can use your dog's current bed)

INSTRUCTIONS:

1   Mark repeat increments on both the T-square ruler and table ruler: 8 inches (20.3 cm) horizontal (staggered at 4 inches [10.2 cm]) and 13 inches (33 cm) vertical.

2   Pin the fabric to your print table and print thickened bleach according to the brick repeat. (For a refresher, see page 80.) Give the bleach up to 30 minutes to oxidize the color. When the fabric lightens to the desired shade, douse it with hydrogen peroxide 3% (I used about one 16-ounce bottle per yard of fabric). Rinse fabric in hot water, wash with Synthrapol, and dry.

3   Cut the panels:

    (a) Two 36 x 30-inch (91.4 x 76.2 cm) top/bottom pieces

    (b) Three 36 x 6-inch (91.4 x 15.2 cm) long side panels, one with Velcro closure

    (c) Two 30 x 6-inch (76.2 x 15.2 cm) short side panels

4   Sew two opposite side panels to the top panel, rights sides together, with a ½-inch (1.3 cm) seam allowance and piping inserted in the seam. **A** Sew the remaining two side panels to the top panel, right sides together, and overlap the piping at the beginning and end.

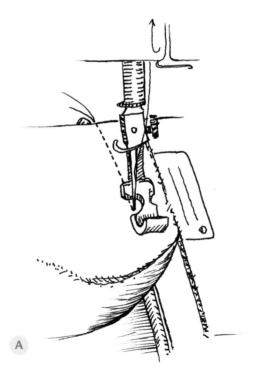

A

5 Fold under 1 inch (2.5 cm) of one long side panel to the wrong side; fold again and press with the iron. Sew the loop side of the Velcro tape to the wrong side of the panel along the fold, leaving a ¼-inch (.6 cm) allowance between the loop tape and the edge of the fold. On the second long panel, fold under 1 inch (2.5 cm) lengthwise and press it back to the wrong side. Sew the fuzzy hook side of the Velcro to the right side of the fold, leaving a ¼-inch (.6 cm) allowance from the fold. Velcro the two pieces together and trim the panel to 6 inches (15.2 cm) high. With right sides together, sew the corners where the two pieces of piping come together, continuing 1 inch (2.5 cm) down the corner seam.

6 Bring the side panels around to sew to the other face panel. Again, sew two parallel sides with the piping between them and then sew the opposites sides, overlapping the piping at the corners. Sew the corners right sides together where the piping overlaps and sew the seams to close them completely. Turn the bed right side out and stuff it with bedding for your dog. **B**

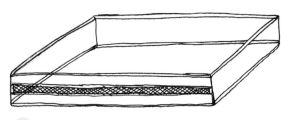

B

YOU WILL NEED:

Scrap fabric with the ribbon motif from your Prize Winner Pet Bed

2 feet (.6 m) of 3/4-inch-wide (1.9 cm) navy blue satin ribbon

2 feet (.6 m) of 1 1/2-inch-wide (3.8 cm) black grosgrain ribbon

Pins

Sewing machine

Navy blue sewing thread

Hand-sewing needle

Pin back

INSTRUCTIONS:

Cut four prize-ribbon circles out of scrap print fabric and stack two together, right sides of each facing up. Cut a V shape from each ribbon end and fold both ribbons in half, placing the fold on top of the stack. Stack the remaining two circles with right sides facing up on top and pin in place. Machine stitch the inner circle around the words Best in Show and the lines radiating out among the "folds" of the ribbon "ruffles" to hold all of the layers together and add some texture and definition. Hand stitch a pin back to the back of the stack. Pin it on your winner's collar. Now that's a proud animal!

KOI STREAMER

For this project, freezer paper makes an ideal stencil because it is easy to cut out multiple, mirrored layers with precision and does not limit size to a screen's print window. Also, it does a great job of resisting the thickened dye, so you can really play with blending colors across the fish's scales and fins for some amazingly festive flyers!

YOU WILL NEED:

Printing surface (page 30)

Tape measure or ruler

Roll of 18-inch-wide (45.7 cm) freezer paper

Scotch tape

Template: page 154

Craft knife

Cutting mat

1 yard (.9 m) of 60-inch-wide (152.4 cm) white woven cotton sheeting per fish

Fabric shears

Iron

Ironing surface, non-padded, like a worktable or the floor

Pins

Thickened, activated dyes in turquoise, red, and yellow (page 99)

Decal spreader or credit card

Steamer and steaming cloths (page 94)

Synthrapol

Sewing machine with universal needle

Neutral-colored sewing thread

Metal ring, 3 inches (7.6 cm) in diameter (a large shower curtain ring works great)

Hand-sewing needle

2 feet (.6 m) white cord or wire, for hanging

INSTRUCTIONS:

1   For each fish, cut two 60-inch (152.4 cm) lengths of freezer paper and tape them together with Scotch tape at the corners with the shiny sides together.

TIP For multiple fish, layer more sheets of freezer paper, their shiny sides paired (I cut six layers at once to make three fish).

2   Center the template on the freezer paper, and tape it in place. Cut out all the black areas with the craft knife on the cutting mat. When you are finished cutting, you will have two mirrored stencils for the two sides of the koi banner.

3   Cut the cotton fabric in half lengthwise to make two 18 x 60-inch (45.7 x 152.4 cm) pieces.

4   Align each stencil on the fabric pieces and iron them down.

5   Pin the stenciled fabrics to the print surface and mix and activate your thickened dyes (see page 99 for a refresher on mixing and activating thickened dyes).

6   Pour the thickened dye on the decal spreader and apply the dye to the fabric. I played with smearing and blending colors—this is the fun part!

7   Cure the dye-printed fabric for 24 hours, then steam for 45 minutes, and wash out excess dyes with Synthrapol (for a refresher on steaming and washing, see pages 103 and 96).

8   Leaving a 1-inch (2.5 cm) seam allowance, cut out the fish silhouettes and the fins separately and place each pair right sides together. Sew each pair of fins right sides together and turn right side out and place inside the seams of the fish silhouettes. Pin in place.

9   Starting at one side of the mouth, sew the fish all the way around to the other side of the mouth. Leave the mouth open and turn the fish right side out. A

10 Insert the metal ring about ¹/₂ inch (1.3 cm) inside fish's mouth and fold the fabric edge down around it and pin. Hand stitch a backstitch through the two thicknesses of fabric to encase the metal ring and finish the fabric hem. Tie a cord on the metal ring from one side of the mouth to the other, hang it in a windy spot, and watch it swim the breeze!

A

WAVES OF GRAIN SCARF

I originally designed this wheat motif for a client who wanted a custom necktie to give to the president of Ukraine. I don't know if the president ever received it, but the tie came out great! I was thrilled to stumble upon the design again and put it into repeat on this scarf. It's easy to dye and print a few scarves at a time; I made a batch of six, each in a different color. With this natural motif, the spacing doesn't have to be precise, so you can eyeball it.

YOU WILL NEED:

Printing surface (page 30)

Template: page 156

Clean, dry, and taped 12 x 16-inch (30.5 x 40.6 cm) screen

14 x 72-inch (35.6 x 182.9 cm) hemmed 100 percent silk scarf (or dye and print a few!)

MX fiber reactive dyes in a few primary colors (page 89)

Vinegar

Small container

Pins

Thiox paste (page 101) (mix right before you print)

Squeegee

Hair dryer

Steamer and steaming cloths (page 94)

Synthrapol

INSTRUCTIONS:

1   Dye each scarf in a small container using less water as described on page 106, using vinegar for the activator for silk. Bunch it into the container and pour two or more colors over it and let it sit for several hours. Hang it to dry overnight so you can print in the morning.

2   Pin the dry scarf on the printing surface, first pinning the corners and then pinning incrementally about every 6 inches (15.2 cm) around the perimeter. Mix your thiox paste to print. Roughly measure (with your eyes) the number of repeats you can make and print every other repeat running along the length of the scarf.

3   Dry the first run of prints with a hair dryer and then print the second run, centering each print between the previous two. Dry each scarf completely, steam it to process the thiox, wash in Synthrapol, and dry. (For a refresher on steaming and washing, see pages 103 and 96).

NIGHT AND DAY QUILT

In my studio, I have two seemingly bottomless scrap bins, one of my hand-dyed silks and one of my hand-printed bamboo jerseys, so it was a no-brainer to harvest from their bounty for this quilt. All the fabrics I used are immersion dyed and screenprinted with thiox. For the large fields of navy blue silks, I printed with thiox (page 101) using the stencil from the Puffy Cloud Pillows (page 110). The finished quilt size is about 45 x 60 inches (114.3 x 152.4 cm).

NOTE *If you are a beginning quilter, I highly recommend using only woven fabrics for this project. I used jersey knits with woven silk, which behave very differently from each other and are technically difficult to combine in a quilt, even for a veteran like myself.*

YOU WILL NEED:

Fabric shears or rotary cutter and cutting mat

About 15 square feet (1.4 square meters) of printed woven fabrics in golden yellow, yellow-green, light blue, and light gray

Sewing machine with universal needle

Sewing thread: light neutral color, black

3 yards (2.7 m) of printed woven fabric in navy blue (I used 55-inch-wide [139.7 cm] silk crepe)

Cotton batting, approximately 50 x 65 inches (127 x 165.1 cm)

Pins (optional)

Hand-sewing needle

Quilting thread: light blue

T-square with ruler for squaring up the quilt

About 6 yards (5.5 m) of light blue bias tape (I cut my own 2 ½-inch-wide [6.4 cm] silk bias strips)

INSTRUCTIONS:

1 Cut scraps and pieces of the golden yellow, yellow-green, light blue, and light gray fabrics into 3-inch-wide (7.6 cm) strips of varying lengths until you have a great big pile of them. If some are narrower or wider, you can group those together as well. I was trying to use even the littlest scraps so a few of my strips were 2 inches (5.1 cm) wide.

2 Arrange the pieces together to form parallel strips on the table or floor. A I started placing the gold tones toward the center and fading out to green and then light blue. If a piece seems out of place, now is a fine time to replace and rearrange it. Keep piecing and placing strips until you have 13 pieced, 62-inch (157.5 cm) vertical columns. With light neutral sewing thread, machine stitch the strips, right sides together, end to end into 62-inch-long (157.5 cm) columns. B Then join the columns, right sides together, side by side.

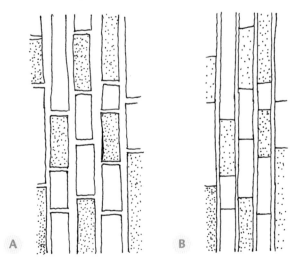

A   B

3   Set aside 2 yards (1.8 m) of navy blue fabric for the
    back. Snip and tear the remaining 1-yard (.9 m) piece
    of dark fabric lengthwise into 3-inch
    (7.6 cm) strips. Sew the strips, right sides together,
    end to end to make nine 62-inch (157.5 cm) vertical
    columns. Sew two columns together side by side,
    right sides facing, and attach to the light pieced field;
    join the remaining seven strips together in the same
    fashion and sew them along the other side of the light
    pieced section. **C**

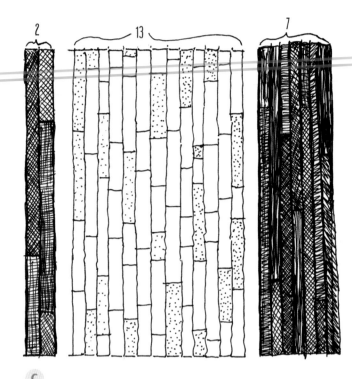

4   Cut the batting an inch or two (2.5 or 5.1 cm) larger
    than the overall dimensions of the quilt top. Piece
    the remainder of the navy blue fabric as necessary
    to make the back of the quilt, which should be also
    be at least an inch or two (2.5 or 5.1 cm) larger than
    the quilt top. Keep it simple with as few pieces
    as possible. Sandwich the three layers together in
    the following order: the quilt back wrong side up, the
    batting, and the quilt top right side up. Starting at
    the center of the quilt, pin (or baste) the entire quilt
    area every few inches.

5   Using light blue quilting thread, hand stitch a par-
    allel running stitch through all three layers of the
    quilt within the seam lines of the light strips as
    shown. **D** Be sure to start and stop stitching about
    2 inches (5.1 cm) from the perimeter of the quilt top;
    this way, when you trim the quilt, you won't cut off
    your knots that hold your stitching in place. If you
    choose to machine quilt the piece, your quilting
    stitches should go all the way to the fabric edge. With
    black sewing thread, machine quilt along the navy
    blue strips with a ¼-inch (.6 cm) allowance from the
    seam between the strips.

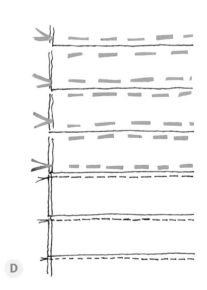

6   Trim the quilt and square up the sides with the
    T-square so all corners are right angles and opposite
    sides are straight and parallel. I trimmed mine to
    60 x 45 inches (152.4 x 114.3 cm) wide.

7   Use commercial bias tape or cut your own and bind
    the quilt. I cut bias tape to 2½ inches (6.4 cm) wide by
    a few inches longer than the entire perimeter of the
    quilt and folded it lengthwise to double it over. Then I
    stitched the binding strip to the front face of the quilt,
    joining the two ends to where they met. I wrapped the
    strip around to the back and hand stitched it in place.

MAIL A MINI MOBILE

This anti e-mail surprise is a fun way to harvest bits of imagery from your scrap fabrics, drop cloths, and masking papers. I wanted to make sure it could be mailed, so I started with the envelope and designed the mobile to fit inside it. Be sure to write the words "Hand Cancel" on the envelope so it doesn't get mangled in a mail-processing machine. Better yet, take it to the post office counter since it might take an extra stamp or two in postage.

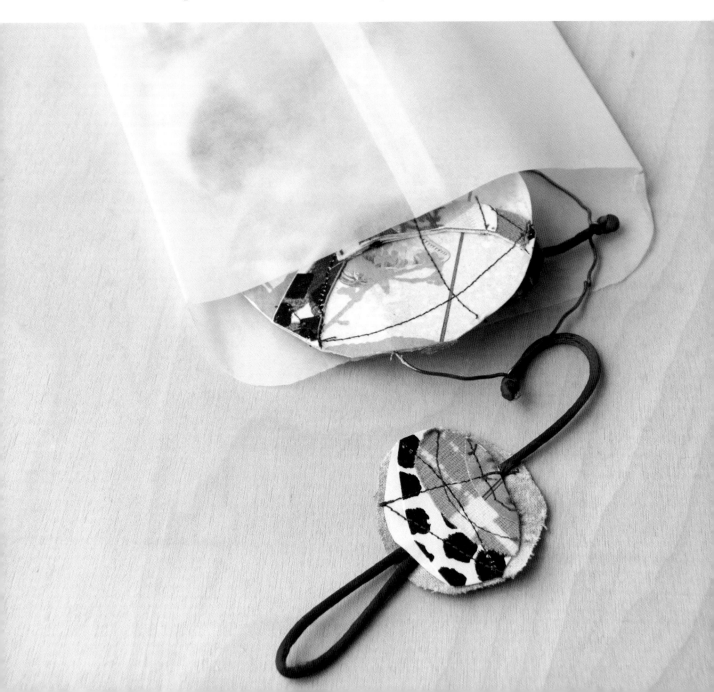

and loop the wire and pull the untied ends of the cord through the loops to the knots.

2   Sandwich the copper between the circles (see below). Iron them between scrap kraft paper to adhere all layers in place.

A

3   Carefully stitch over the circles to better secure the layers. I recommend slowly moving the needle with the hand wheel as you pass over the copper wire to avoid hitting it and breaking a needle. Trim the sewing threads.

4   Artfully arrange and glue a few decorative scrap printing pieces on the envelope and mail it to your lucky recipient!

YOU WILL NEED:

Scissors

Scraps from printing: drop cloths, scrap fabrics, and masking papers

Template: page 157

Sewable, lightweight iron-on, paper-backed adhesive

About 2 feet (.6 m) of red cord (cut from the spool in the cord and ribbon section at the fabric store)

Needle-nose pliers

Copper wire

Iron and ironing board

Kraft paper

Sewing machine with universal needle

Sewing thread in accent color

6 x 9-inch (15.2 x 22.9 cm) manila envelope for mailing

Scotch tape

INSTRUCTIONS:

1   Cut out your favorite print scraps and arrange them back-to-back in five pairs according to the templates. On the back of one of the circles in each pair, attach paper-backed adhesive and peel off the adhesive's backing paper. Cut and knot the red cord according to the illustration. A Use the needle-nose pliers to cut

TEMPLATES

PUFFY CLOUD PILLOWS

(page 110) *enlarge 250%*

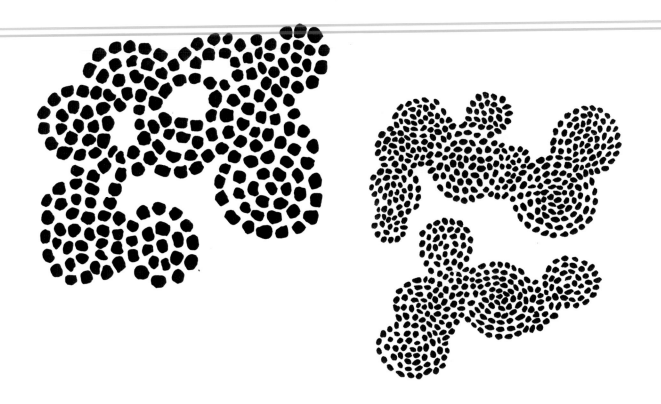

BICYCLE BEACH TOTE

(page 122) *enlarge 200%*

Game Board Frame

TRAVEL BACKGAMMON SET

(page 116) *shown at 100%*

Backgammon Triangles

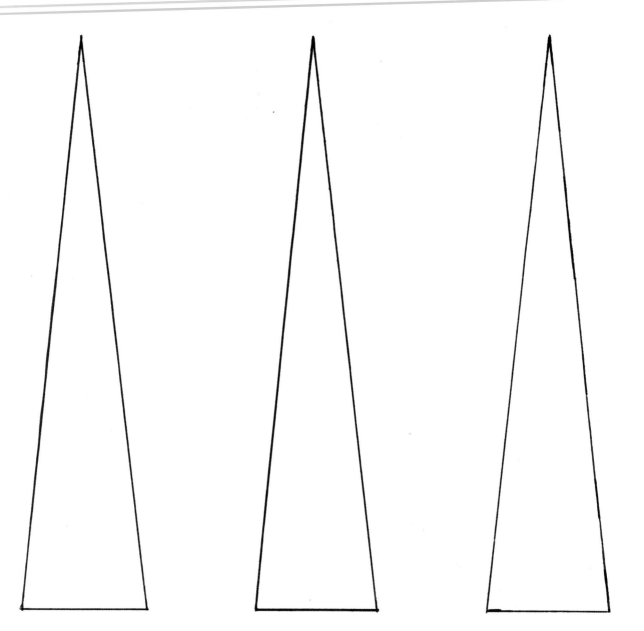

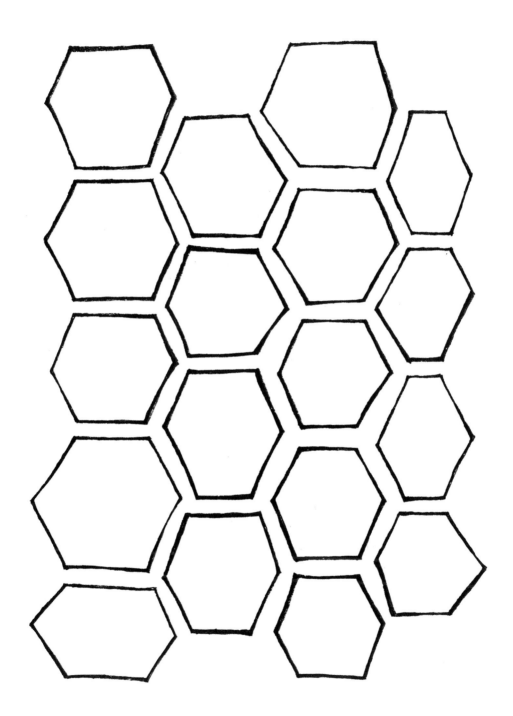

FERRIS WHEEL SKIRT

(page 124) *enlarge 250%*

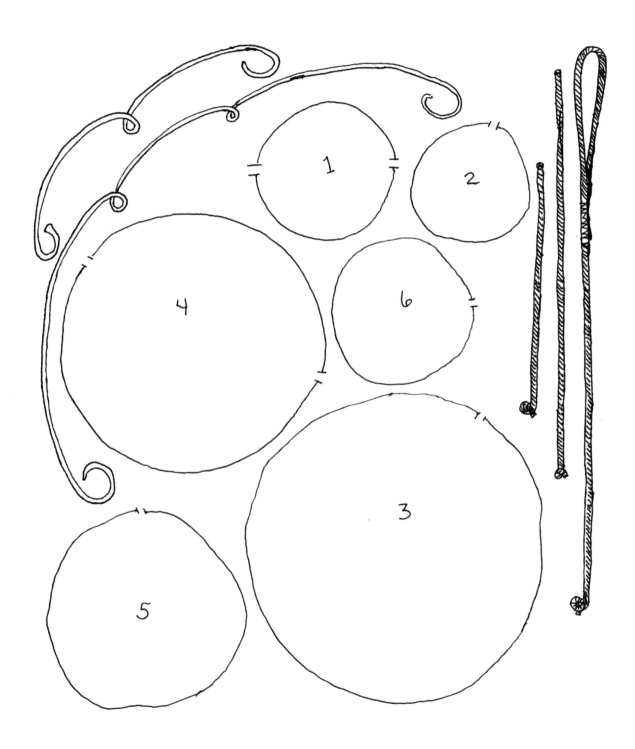

RESOURCES

You can pick up general materials and supplies, like vinegar and contact paper, at your local grocery store or home improvement store. Score fun fabrics, clothing, and other inspiring, printable treasures at thrift stores and yard sales (remember to prewash them!). For the more specialized, print-specific supplies and PFD (prepared for dyeing) fabrics, it's easier to order online or by phone and watch them arrive at your door.

Keep a few factors in mind when browsing suppliers' catalogs and websites:

URGENCY: My husband often tells me, "Don't sweat the truck." Ground shipping is cheaper than air, economy turnaround is cheaper than rush service, and having ordered your materials last week is far more efficient (and reassuring) than frantically driving all around town trying to find something comparable last minute.

QUANTITY: The old adage is true: you can get it cheaper by the dozen, especially from my favorite suppliers listed at right. This goes for anything from sewing-machine needles and silk scarves to gallons of base extender and rolls of kraft paper. If you can't quite swing the up-front expense of buying in bulk, go in on a larger quantity with a friend or colleague and split the shipping costs, too.

GEOGRAPHY: In-state retail purchases are subject to sales tax, which, on top of shipping, adds significantly to your cost. Of course, with ordering something from across state lines, you won't be subject to sales tax, but you will have to pay for shipping. Be sure to find out where your order is shipping from: the closer the warehouse, the quicker and cheaper it will arrive at your door.

SCREENPRINTING SUPPLIES

Victory Factory
Hollis, NY
www.victoryfactory.com
(800) 255-5335

Welsh Products, Inc.
Berkeley, CA
www.diyprintsupply.com
(800) 745-3255

GENERAL ART SUPPLIES

Blick Art Supplies
Galesburg, IL
www.dickblick.com
(800) 828-4548

Pearl Paint Fine Art Supplies
Fort Lauderdale, FL
www.pearlpaint.com
(800) 451-7327

TEXTILE ART AND CRAFT SUPPLIES

Dharma Trading Company
San Rafael, CA
www.dharmatrading.com
(800) 542-6227

Jacquard Products
Healdsburg, CA
www.jacquardproducts.com
(800) 442-0455

Pro Chemical and Dye
Somerset, MA
www.prochemicalanddye.com
(800) 228-9393

SEWING SUPPLIES

WAWAK
Endwell, NY
www.wawak.com
(800) 654-2235

Sew True
New York, NY
www.sewtrue.com
(800) 739- 8783

OTHER SUPPLIES

ULINE
Pleasant Prairie, WI
www.uline.com
(800) 958-5463

FREE DOWNLOADABLE CLIP ART

The Graphics Fairy, LLC
www.graphicsfairy.blogspot.com

Wikimedia Commons
www.commons.wikimedia.org

ABOUT THE AUTHOR

Jen Swearington is an independent designer and artist. In 2003, she founded Jennythreads Studio and since then has made her living creating handmade, hand-printed apparel and accessories. She has also exhibited in Quilt National three times, winning the Award of Excellence in 2009. She has taught at the Savannah College of Art and Design, the University of North Carolina at Asheville, Penland School of Crafts, and Arrowmont School of Arts and Crafts. Originally from Indiana, she lives in the mountains of North Carolina with her husband, two dogs, and two cats. See what she's up to these days at www.jennythreads.net.

ACKNOWLEDGMENTS

This book is dedicated to my aunts Kelly, Janice, and Mary.

A million thanks to the surprisingly good-natured individuals who were right there with me (and my many freak-outs) through my first book, a frequently overwhelming project:

My dreamy husband, Paul Walker, true love and one-man support team, who keeps up my strength with chocolate doughnuts and cherry soda.

My sharp editor, Thom O'Hearn, who creates order from my abundant chaos and brightens our correspondence with a well-placed :)

My sunny assistant, Ashley Cole, who valiantly copilots the "SS Jennythreads" while talking me out of jumping overboard.

And my patient, encouraging friends and family, who watch me disappear and resurface in their lives between far too many projects and deadlines, again and again.

Special thanks to Valerie Van Arsdale Shrader, whose guidance led one morning's idea to becoming this book.

INDEX